The
Dope Game
Misadventures of
Fat Cat & Pappy
Mason

THE MOST INFAMOUS STREET LEGENDS OUT OF HIP-HOP'S LYRICAL LORE

SETH FERRANTI

Gorilla Convict Publications © 2014
ISBN 978-0-9889760-1-6
eBook ISBN 978-0-9889760-1-6

Printed in the United States of America
First Printing February 2014

Published by
Gorilla Convict Publications
1019 Willott Road
St. Peters, MO 63376
www.gorillaconvict.com

"During the past decade, Seth Ferranti has become a master story teller, historian and chronicler of the street legends largely spawned by drug prohibition." Ron Chepesiuk, author of Escobar vs Cali and Sergeant Smack

"In his new book, Ferranti has, from behind bars, published his masterpiece, an amazing study of one brutal and vicious but legendary gang's dominance of the crack trade during a new era in the history of the black gangster where art and the streets intersected to shape the growing hip-hop culture." amazon.com

"If you like gangster stories, true crime, hip-hop or New York culture, this is a great read. I will definitely be reading more of Seth Ferranti's work and I have to say more authors like him are needed. He's already a force, but once he's released I believed we will go from seeing his name on pages to in credits. Hopefully on an unfiltered HBO type of series." Mobb Bunny23, amazon.com

"Another great book from Seth Ferranti with page turning, raw uncut details about some of the coldest crews and cats out there. Highly recommended to anyone that is into books about true crime." Kindle Edition, amazon.com

"This is not sensationalized writing about what goes on in the streets but very well written and researched journalism that goes in-depth into the genesis and environments that created these men. If you want to know what the streets of urban American produce, I suggest you read this book." Black TK, Larceny Media

"Seth Ferranti is the real deal. His books are serious. They tell the sides of things you don't see in the movies. The bad side of gangster life and what it involves as well as the good. This book is a must read for anyone who likes this genre of books." amazon. com

"Ferranti writes like the gangsters speak. His books give a voice that is far different than just a historical recitation. Really well done work for fans of street level true crime." Scott M. Deitche, author of Rogue Mobster

"Take a ride with Seth Ferranti as he gathers knowledge from interviews, testimonials of how and why these young men become the epitome of their city. This book profiles each legend during the crack epidemic and how each one is on one accord with the no snitching movement during their reign in the streets." Readers Paradise Book Club

"I remember watching New Jack City as a kid and feeling like it was a fantasy similar to Avatar or Alice in Wonderland, thinking no gang could be as ruthless, as determined, and as exciting as the CMB. Truth be told, I think the exploits of Fat Cat and his crew far upstage any fictionalized account that could be conceived in Hollywood. The book digs into the origin and really gives you a look into the mind of the drug lords more so than watching American Gangster or listening to a few rap songs." amazon.com

"Seth creates the perfect balance of admiration and consequences for these street legends. The moral of the story is that crime does not pay, but it does make for one hell of a read." The Pen

"It is a war report live and direct from behind enemy lines. Raw and uncut. I recommend this to anyone who is looking to get more knowledge on American gangsters and how they operate." amazon.com

"Seth Ferranti brings clarity to the chaos and pulls you in with him showing the allegiances, hierarchies and threats that exist in the streets. I was gripped and you should read this." amazon.com

"The sheer violence and brutality of the book exposes the reader to the harsh environment that exists within the inner-cities and is an alarming wake up call to the kill or be killed mentality that exists." barnesandnoble.com

To all my fans, thank you for making my writings a success. To my wife Diane, thank you for making my dreams come true from behind these fences. To the streets, thanks for keeping it real and showing the world what it's really like.

"I'm from Queens/Pappy and Fat Cat/Supreme Team/ South Jamaica cats that." Reminisce '03, Mr. Cheeks featuring Pete Rock and CL Smooth, Back Again (2003)

"I might be super nigger." George Jackson

"In this world, violence is a voice of reason like that of America's praised gunslingers: Billy the Kid or Jesse James and other killers who wear the taking of life like a badge of honor." Nannon Williams

"In reality, the criminal code is no more than an eclectic mix of moral etiquette borrowed from such diverse sources as the Knights of the Round Table, the Japanese code of Bushido and Hollywood westerns." Razor Smith

"History understands only big things." Jack Henry Abbot

"Political power grows out of the barrel of a gun." Chairman Mao

The
Dope Game
Misadventures of
Fat Cat & Pappy Mason

The Southside of Jamaica Queens, home to multi-platinum rappers like 50 Cent and Nas and legendary drug lords like Fat Cat and Pappy Mason, has become ground zero for hip-hop hustlers, rap culture and urban drug thugs. The borough that bred some of the most progressive, notorious and brutal gangsters of the 20th century, has gone down in street mythology as a central part of gangsta rap's lyrical lore. Dudes that were on that Al Capone, John Gotti, Mafia-type level, carved out their niche with a deadly effectiveness in the black underworld of the Southside. Handling their business and leaving fear in the hearts of suckers everywhere, the hustlers from Queens epitomized what the word gangster meant.

During the mid-1980s crack explosion the drug barons had the ultimate power. With mountains of cash, an arsenal of weapons and a ruthless abandon that granted them an unrivaled respect, they became legends that were both iconic and infamous in their own time. They gravitated toward and acquired the material items that came to define hip-hop's bling-bling lifestyle in the late 1990s- the luxury cars, the jewelry, the clothes, the money, the accessories and the girls- everything that inner-city residents of capitalistic America considered trappings of success. In the era of Reaganomics, the dope lords were the Don's of the ghetto. Not afraid to flaunt their wealth, power and glory for the whole world to see.

Fat Cat and his partner Pappy Mason were the stars of the dope show in the 1980s. They led an organized and disciplined drug dealing crew in the South Jamaica, Queens neighborhood of New York City, that has proved unmatched in the chronicles of gangster lore. The gang sold a variety of drugs and cleared as much as $100,000 per week in profit. In a time dominated by the Italian Mafia, Fat Cat and Pappy Mason got theirs in a bold, brutal and brash style, with the class, swagger and dignity of true hustlers, born to the hood.

During one of the most violent epochs in New York City's history, Fat Cat and Pappy Mason held serve to endure a long and successful run in the often deadly and volatile dope game. Influencing both the hustlers of the day, as well as the emerging rap superstars and burgeoning industry figures. Hip-hop and hustling were worlds apart in stature, but their denizens shared the same neighborhoods. Growing up in the same projects, they all congregated down on the block and socialized within the same circles. Intermingling, exchanging ideas and embracing a culture that would explode internationally by the early-90s.

But when hip-hop started, street guys like Fat Cat and Pappy Mason, were the true stars. They were the ones holding court like royalty. They embodied the spirit of the anti-hero outlaws that hip-hop romanticized. And the truth of it was they considered the upstart rappers soft, but they supported the movement, watching as their homeboys made the rap game a viable industry, creating a whole new genre in the process. Still, the part the drug thugs played in hip-hop is undeniable.

A generation of rappers and hip-hop executives grew up under street stars like Fat Cat and Pappy Mason. They emulated the mentality, attitudes and mindset of the drug lords. And when hip-hop hit the big time, the stories of the crack era hustlers became a permanent part of hip-hop mythology and history. Elevating street legends like Fat Cat and Pappy Mason to iconic status in popular culture and making them modern day criminal celebrities. Through the power and growth of hip-hop, the hood legends of Queens rivaled outlaw heroes like Billy the Kid, Pablo Escobar and Whitey Bulger. Imprinting a vivid image of the black gangster in our national consciousness, that thrives today in Hollywood, music and entertainment circles.

CHAPTER 1
The Jump Off

Dedicated to niggas like Fat Cat and Pappy Mason/I do this
for the gangsters man/All we got is us, Noreaga, Reunion
(2000)

Lorenzo "Fat Cat" Nichols was born on December 25th, 1958 in Birmingham, Alabama. A Christmas baby, he was the fourth child to join the Nichols family. His mother worked long hours as a nurse's aid, cleaning bed pans and assisting staff at a local hospital. His father was a factory supervisor. As the youngest and only boy, Lorenzo received lots of attention from all the women in his family, especially his maternal grandmother. Growing up around his grandmother, Lorenzo had his first exposure to illegal activity.

"My grandmother was known for selling bootleg liquor and running card games." Cat said. "To me it seemed normal." Violence was also an essential part of his early years, shaping his future disposition and outlook on life. One time his parent's fighting got so bad it resulted in his father getting shot in the ass. "I was too young to remember the details, but I was told my pops put his hands on her during an argument and she went for her gun." Cat said nonchalantly, exposing his gangster upbringing.

Eventually Cat's mother left Alabama and his father for New York City, leaving Cat to be raised by his grandmother. He would journey north to visit his mother every summer in New York, but Cat preferred living with his grandmother in Alabama. When his mother settled and got remarried though, she sent for her son.

"They told me I was only going for the summer, but when school started I knew what it was." Cat said. City life would impact Cat's teenage years in drastic ways. "He was sent to live with his mother at 139th and Linden in South Ozone Park in Queens. His mother worked as a nursing maid, his stepfather a plumber." Lance Fuertado, a Queens native said. "He was definitely good by nature, but he was a tough kid."

Queens wasn't considered hard, in fact it was semi-middle class, but it was still the hood, even if it didn't look the part. As the new kid on the block, Cat was challenged immediately by his peers and he responded in kind. "Lots of fistfights, no gunplay. He got the name Fat Cat for his sturdy physique." Curtis Scoon, a producer for BET's American Gangster series said. In essence, Cat could go all UFC on someone.

"I was a wild child," Cat said. "I was acting out because I didn't really want to be in New York." His wilding out and ability with his fists attracted several admirers in his new locale. He quickly befriended his neighbors- Tony, Todd and Lance Fuertado, and the slightly older Michael Mitchell, who everyone called Black.

In 1972, Black formed the Queens division of the Seven Crowns, a gang originally from the Bronx. Cat and Pretty Tony joined the Lil' Crowns and Cat quickly became their enforcer. "Cat was big and strong for his age," Black said. "Smart kid too, and on top of that, he was good with his hands. We were the ones who gave him the name Fat Cat, because of his size."

They called the stump like, five-foot-eight, 230 pound man-child Fat Cat. The nickname had more to do with Nichols' reputation than build. Fat Cat's sister, Viola, knew the hyperactive teenager by another name. She called him

"Busy." Because as a child he was into everything.

Cat started his career in the Seven Crowns robbing stores. The Crowns dabbled in heroin and pot, but specialized in robberies. Cat was known as a strong arm, more than happy to use force to implement his will. He moved from robbing stores to robbing a bar and a supermarket. "They robbed Wonder Bread trucks," Curtis Scoon said. Cat worked on the side stealing car radios too.

He was also a top flight b-ball guard in high school. He balanced school, home and street life, but eventually went into the streets full time and when he did, he was like the ocean. No talking, all action. "Any dispute between the Crowns and another gang to be settled in a one on one fashion, Cat was the fighter." D, a dude who grew up with Cat says. A detective from the era remembered his first interaction with Cat.

"I first met Fat Cat when we went into the Forty's Houses to break up the Seven Crowns. They didn't call him Fat Cat then. They called him Fat Boy. Any problems in the gang and they called in Nichols to crush it. There were only twelve of us in the whole task force, so you got to know the street players pretty well. The Crowns had their drugs, but it was mostly smoke and heroin. No cocaine to speak of. Certainly no crack. Only the white kids were fucking around with angel dust. The same with pills. The Crowns wouldn't screw around with pills. Fat Cat was just a kid, but he was a big kid. He had a mouth on him too. Still, he had some magnetism. You could see that.

"If we wanted guys to move, we'd go to Fat Cat. Once the Cat moved, they'd all follow. The gangs were very territorial. The Seven Crowns weren't allowed up on Hillside and Parsons. The Latin Soul Brothers weren't allowed to go down past South Road. Shit like that. The blacks weren't allowed to go over 102nd Avenue where the Sex Boys were. Sex Boys were white guys. They were a bullshit gang. The big thing back then was wearing colors. Nobody really had guns yet. The fighting was mostly hand-to-hand stuff. Occasionally you'd see a knife or a homemade zip gun. All we basically did was go and harass the gangs." The detective said.

"We were just friends. This is how everything came together. It was one love. We were unified. This is like 77-78," Lance Fuertado said. The Seven Crowns, with its strong personalities like Fat Cat, was a force in the ghetto. All the teenagers wanted to be down and be a part of the clique. The gangs were neighborhood cliques of kids at the time, but they would evolve into serious criminal organizations.

In Queens, the gangs' leaders became de-facto shotcallers. They ran the hood and their word became law. Certain community leaders tried to get the Crowns to use their influence in a positive way. They recognized the brotherhood the gang embodied and sought to utilize it for the greater good. But it wasn't happening; the young hustlers had their own plan.

"Ask anybody from the neighborhood- Cat, Lance, Tony- they were the dudes bonded by the Crowns like brothers." Raheim, Cat's son said. This bond solidified the gang's future in the drug game. As close friends, who grew up together, their loyalty was unquestioned and paramount to the foundation of the organizations they would form.

"Originally we started out as kids- me, Tony, Lance, Cat. We went from robberies to selling drugs to stealing cars to everything." Big Hen, Cat's brother-in-law said. The gang started out stealing, whatever they could get their hands on and selling marijuana, then graduated to heroin. It was a natural progression in the ways of criminality.

"I always knew about Fat Cat cause of Seven Crowns." Shocker, an original member of the Bebos says. "Seven Crowns was a big known gang in my neighborhood." Youthful days of robbery and weed dealing established Cat's reputation as a formidable gang member. But he earned his stripes in the criminal underworld for serious offenses such as assault, armed robbery and attempted murder. "Cat was a brawler, he could fight. He was arrested several times as a teenager." Curtis Scoon said. And when arrested Cat proved he belonged by keeping his mouth shut. By adhering to the street code, Fat Cat solidified his credentials as an up-and-coming gangster. In the eyes of the underworld he had unlimited potential.

Cat was arrested for the first time as an adult in 1976, and charged with possession of stolen property. In his seventeenth year, Cat was arrested four times for weapons possession and larceny. He was sentenced in 1977 to juvy, after holding up a bar in Queens at gunpoint. He landed in Spofford Youth House, where he met his future partner-in-crime, Howard "Pappy" Mason, a young tough from Brooklyn.

Spofford Youth House was a place for rebellious, delinquent kids. It was the place where they sent the worst of the worst- the incorrigible, the violent, the hard cases. The juvenile facility was not prison, but for the young teenagers it held, it might as well have been Alcatraz. Some adapted, some didn't. It was a dog-eat-dog kind of place. Alpha males like Fat Cat used it as a stepping stone to their future aspirations in the criminal underworld, by making connections, showing what they were about and networking.

Criminals found those with like minds and this was the case with Cat and Pap. Pappy Mason and Fat Cat found they shared Alabama roots, and a desire to use violence to solve their problems, although Pappy seemed to prefer fighting the authorities. The two would hit it off and become lifelong friends. Forming a fraternity based on crime and getting busy.

"Pap was a motherfucker to have on your team and Cat knows it," D says. "Them two dudes loved each other." Both Cat and Pappy believed in the, "I'm my brother's keeper" mentality, long before *New Jack City* made the maxim popular. They would "do or die" for each other and this loyalty served them well.

Pappy Mason was the youngest of six children born to Claudia Mason in Montgomery, Alabama. The Mason's relocated to Brooklyn while Pappy was young and lived on Troy Avenue, between President and Union Streets, in the Crown Heights section of Brooklyn. The area was heavily populated with Jamaicans. Bing from the Supreme Team confirms this. "Pappy Mason was from Brooklyn, Crown Heights, not Queens."

He says. By the age of 13, Pap became a member of the Jolly Stompers, a local street gang.

"There's not a lot of history on this dude. They say this nigga was from the Brook, from Brooklyn somewhere." BC, a Queens native from the era says. "Pap was a Brooklyn cat, Crown Heights/ Troy Avenue area." Brooklyn was known for having that thug-shit on lock back then. Of the five boroughs, the BK was known for producing the most thorough and grimy dudes. Dudes that would befriend you and rob you without a thought.

"People may say that all hoods are the same," Dex, a Brooklyn native from the era says. "But I been through a lot of different states and none of them compare to New York. Where I had to always be on point in New York, in those other states I could see everything that was coming my way easily. It's all about making money and stayed strapped in them streets of Crooklyn. Can't trust no one because everyone is on some cut-throat shit trying to come up by any means necessary. You earn your respect by busting your gun, or your ass was going to get eaten alive."

In this environment Pappy became a fighter, who was tested in Brooklyn's vicious street culture everyday and versed on how to be a man in the boroughs' rough projects. "Pappy liked to fight a lot," Curtis Scoon said. "Him and Cat bonded over their abilities to knock motherfuckers out."

The five-foot-eight Pappy had a pit bull mindset and would just as soon look at someone, as punch them in the face. The kid didn't take no shorts. He was feisty, aggressive and ruthless. Vicious as a wild dog and ready to attack. This attitude endeared him to Cat, who saw in Pappy, a man after his own heart.

Pap started his criminal career as a stick-up kid. He was the crazy dude that crazy dudes thought twice about. "Pappy was like a grenade without a pin." A dude from the era says. "He wasn't known as a drug player, but as a hothead who hated police." Pap would tell cops "suck my dick" to their face, and he routinely held up his big middle finger to authority. That was just how he was cut.

To Pappy, the police were white devils who held the black

man in oppression. Being from Alabama, Pappy had that anti-slavery mentality. He had a problem with authority figures from the jump and his preferred way of handling that problem was with his fists. He had no problem getting busy and that defiant stance would come to define him.

Much of his formative years were spent in and out of juvenile facilities such as Spofford and Warwick. As he grew older his criminal activities advanced, earning him stays at Rikers Island and an assortment of state penitentiaries like Attica and Comstock. Going to jail was just part of the game to Pappy. He was a criminal who stuck to the street code, and he expected anyone associated with him to keep their mouths shut also.

"A lot of people confuse what the measure of a man is, because in different contexts, it takes on different meanings," D says. "We have people in this world that from all outward appearances are doing the right thing, but have no integrity. Conversely, you have people in this world, that according to society, are doing all the wrong things, yet they have the most integrity. That is Pappy Mason."

Pappy's disposition was so bad behind bars that he forfeited all of his good time on a three-to-seven year sentence. He served everyday on seven years, something that was unheard of during that time. "Pappy is the only person I know back then who had seven years and did everyday of it. He left owing nothing." Fat Cat said. Pap's friendship with Cat was solid, but neither had a clue how that friendship would affect each other and countless others in the future.

"Cat was a serious guy. If you were cool with him, you were alright." D says. Cat spent two-and-a-half years in state prison and came out on parole in January 1980. "Cat served time for armed robbery and came home at 21." D says. "Cat had gone into juvie bad and came out of prison worse. He'd already shown that he could intimidate people on the street, and that gave him a good start in the drug business."

Cat went to work for Ronnie Bumps, the local drug lord, almost immediately. From Ronnie Bumps, he learned the value of discretion and good connections. The elder gangster was a mentor of sorts for the young "G", but Cat also had his Seven Crown's contacts. "Growing up in Queens, we were involved in a lot of activities. We wreaked a lot of havoc in our community." Lance Fuertado said, and all the activity was centered around the block.

CHAPTER 2

The Block

Fat Cat would become somewhat of an enforcer, because he was big for his size and knew how to use his fists. Cat would whip many a ass and stay in trouble. As Is Magazine, Issue 3.

When Cat was paroled in 1980, the Queens streets he returned to were unfamiliar. Slinging coke had become the routine and his childhood friend Pretty Tony was deep in the game. "Tony was a smart dude, a real good businessman." Cat said.

Tony Fuertado was a Spanish cat getting money. They called him Pretty Tony because he was smooth with the ladies. It was said women were attracted to him like a moth to a flame. Like Cat, Pretty Tony was a Seven Crowns alumni, who was moving on to bigger and better things. He had seen the future and that future was drugs. Pretty Tony and his brother Lance were down on the block hustling.

"The block back then was 150th Street," Shocker says. "There'd be hustlers everywhere. You had junkies and coke fiends lined up like they were giving out free cheese." With so much clientele there was enough money for everybody. Cat figured with his homeboys down on the block, he would join them. They were learning how to move and showed Cat the game.

"Back then the game was the game. Everybody stood by the rules. Soldiers were soldiers." Bing says. Between Ronnie Bumps and the Fuertado brothers, Cat was getting a Master's degree in the drug game. He became a serious student of narcotics and started living the hustler's life. His game point average was modest, but Cat had serious potential.

"Due to the numbers of the Crowns, over 1000, they dealt primarily in coke and heroin. Some weed too," Curtis Scoon said. "From what Fat Cat told me, he would get a pound for about $450 and when he broke it down into $5 bags, he could make about $1500 and he was doing this when he hit the street. He was somebody you had to respect with his brain power and his muscle. A big shootout at a skating rink made his name."

There was a beef between Fat Cat and an already established crew called the Corleys over territory. "They was at this skating rink on Jamaica Avenue, the Corley crew and Fat Cat crew got into a shootout. Then after that Corley and Fat Cat must have come to some kind of agreement, cause Fat Cat got a spot in Forty Projects, which was a Corley stronghold." Shocker says. "We hustled in Forty on one end and Wall Corely's people had the other end of Forty." Cat was expanding his operations.

"A lot of shootings occurred in Forty Projects. If they didn't know then, they knew now to what extent Fat Cat would go to." D says. With the skating rink incident and the encroachment on another crew's turf, Cat was showing his gangster. Fat Cat was a gunman/fighter/thinker/manipulator - all in one person. He made his name out on the block doing him, then consolidated.

"I remember walking down the block when I was a shorty and I used to be scared to death," BC says. "I would see mad people on the block doing their thing. I didn't know exactly what was poppin' cause I was naive to the fact, but I knew illegal shit was poppin'." One Hundred Fiftieth Street, between South Road and 107th, was where the block was located. It became an open air drug bazaar, where anything could be had, for a price.

"Fat Cat made that block infamous and it will forever be known as the block." BC says. On parole and under the guidance of Ronnie Bumps and Pretty Tony, Cat organized what would become a six-figure a day drug enterprise. "Fat Cat was truly a chess player. Strictly business, he had enforcers." Ethan Brown, who wrote *Queens Reigns Supreme* said. One of Cat's first suppliers was Ronnie Bumps.

Cocaine found a boom market in Queens. Colombian dealers were pouring into Jackson Heights, killing people by the dozens and selling kilos to all comers. Bumps, who was buying kilos directly from the Colombians, had cornered the market, but when he was arrested on a federal indictment for drug trafficking in Baltimore, Fat Cat was ready to take the crown. He was more than ready, he was extremely capable. He seized power in a bloodless succession.

As Nichols' reputation grew so did his waistline. Slowly but surely, he became a kind of Robin Hood figure. Cat ran his organization according to a familiar business model. He looked to his predecessors for guidance. Like the Frank Lucas and Nicky Barnes' heroin operations of the 70s, Fat Cat's small army of drug dealers were grinding, making dozens of small transactions a day on the block worth $10 to $25 each. It was strictly a retail business. Profits were sizable, but the rank and file dealers had to work fifteen hour days.

"Cat had already started getting money. He was pushing a 98, wearing Adidas and had a lot of fat jewels. He weighed a good 300 pounds, and he would be on the block with mopeds lined up for his people." Luc "Spoon" Stephens, a dude from Cat's crew said. "I would get change from him. I was getting my hustle on, so I would get hundred dollar bills from him. He noticed that and wanted to know who I was, coming for change everyday. He asked my name and we started kicking it.

"Time went on and he put me on. He put me on under this dope fiend named Head. I got my work, finished my pack and go to re-up and Head ain't nowhere around. Probably somewhere high, so I tell Cat and he's like 'Okay, I'm a hit you myself.' So he gives me three grams. Back then dope could take an 80, but I would just put on a 40. I think it was $1200 then. I would hit the block with my man Nut and get loose. I'd do $1200 and then some more, and Cat decided I needed to be down."

Cat slowly started forming his crew around him. "Jughead, Bobo, Luc, they was really like a family." Shocker says. "Fat Cat was pushing whatever he wanted. He changed cars like nigga's changed clothes. I remember one time Fat Cat's man was driving one of his brand new cars. Actually it was a Porsche and he wrecked the car and the very next day Fat Cat rode down my project with another brand new car. He had all the cars/jewelry."

On the street, Nichols was gaining attention. His nickname started to be more a tribute to his influence in the community than a reference to his size. "He wasn't fat, just large," said one neighbor. He would often be found on a corner of 150th Street observing the action. He was also a familiar sight in St. Albans and Springfield Gardens wearing an expensive array of chains and a rabbit fur coat, often driving an Audi.

He started sponsoring a neighborhood basketball league and outfitted his players in matching t-shirts and sneakers. College stars like Walter Berry, Pearl Washington and Mark Jackson played in the drug league games. The action courtside could get crazy though. "You couldn't keep what was happening out in the street from moving onto the playground," Fly Williams, a former ABA star said. Shootings and beatdowns were a regular at the events. It was all part of the spectacle.

Nichols was, first and foremost, a gang leader. He referred to everyone in his crew as homes, short for homeboy, and it was not uncommon for the Cat to lead his homeboys in a jog around the neighborhood. In a community devoid of heroes, Cat became a pervase role model. He would often be seen on the edges of 150th Street handing out money to kids. He also gave advice on food and exercise.

After blowing up to over 300 pounds, he went on a mean diet and exercise routine to get back in shape. The Cat was a man of extremes and his discipline was as legendary as his disregard for it. He had a big heart though. He took busloads of kids to Great Adventures amusement park and footed the bill for several weekend barbecues in Baisley Park.

"In every hood people make a name for themselves," Bing says and the Cat was no different. He had the jewelry, the clothes, the women, the gold and the cars. In Queens, Fat Cat was someone to emulate. "Fat Cat was a man among boys, the hustler of hustlers. He was getting crazy money." Shocker says.

Word of the bustling drug trade on 150th Street made it a magnet for both up-and-coming entrepreneurs and seasoned tough guys. By the time Pappy Mason came home in 1983, from his most recent stint in prison, Fat Cat was already established as a major force in the drug trade in Queens. Pap sought Cat out looking for a job and Cat hired him as security with a salary of $1000 a week.

Pap's no nonsense attitude and loyalty quickly got him noticed, and he moved up the organizational hierarchy quickly. In no time, Pappy was given the spot in Forty Projects. The drug trade treated Fat Cat's crew good, they were ghetto superstars, and Fat Cat and Pappy were like Batman and Robin.

"Fat Cat and them were working out of the middle building I used to hang around." Shocker says. "We hustled in the project like outside. I'd guess you'd say that was the spot, Fat Cat gave Pap the spot. Shit, everyone was getting paid." In the beginning it was all about getting money, later that would change.

"When you hear Cat, you hear Pap." BC says of the pair. Pap emerged as Cat's man in the streets. Cat knew Pap had mad heart and was fiercely loyal. Pappy took his job serious too; he did it with a vengeance. "He was feared, loved, respected, looked up to and highly regarded. A lot of people thought he was crazy and not to be fucked with." Shocker says.

With his Rastafarian style dreadlocks and an acquired Jamaican patios, Mason added further mystique to his already fearsome and foreboding presence. His viciousness and image enhanced his already tough reputation. Dudes thought he was from Jamaica, an exotic and foreign gangster that Cat had imported over to protect his interests.

"Pappy grew up in Crown Heights, Brooklyn, which had a large Jamaican population," the Pathfinder says. "Most of his friends were either Jamaicans or from the islands. As someone who actually met Pappy in 1983, my impression of him was a quiet reserved brother who didn't say much. I could tell he wasn't a follower. It was only when he spoke about the prison system that he opened up. The friend who introduced me to Pappy was also American, but I considered him Jamaican because he spoke the patios as well as I did and I'm Jamaican. In the 1980s there was a Jamaican/Caribbean movement going on throughout the five boroughs where it was cool to act and sound Jamaican."

Pappy had a strong aura surrounding him. Because of his dreadlocks and his use of Jamaican street slang, street guys in both Brooklyn and Queens believed he was part of a deadly Jamaican posse, when in fact, like Fat Cat, he was from Alabama. "Pap's got a good heart, if he's your friend, he's your friend. But if he's your enemy, that's something altogether different." D says.

The enforcer for Cat's crew formed his own crew. The Bebos grew dreads and sold cocaine and heroin in Forty Projects. "The Bebos were underneath Pap. He was the head nigga in charge. He was amongst them Bebo niggas from Forty Projects." BC says. Along with the dreadlocks, Pap's crew emulated him in all matters, from his violent ways to his speech patterns.

"They used to try and be like Pap, talking Jamaican and the like. A lot of dudes were under Pap. He had a strong influence in our hood." BC says. "Bebo is short for who you be, bro. These guys were very suspicious. Pappy went by that name when he talked on the phone. It was Bebo this and Bebo that. He got all them kids in the Forty's talking Jamaican."

Pappy installed in his subordinates an obsession with Jamaican culture. Like their boss, Bebo members framed orders for everything from cocaine shipments to hits on potential witnesses with the Rastafarian phrase, "one love." Pappy and the Bebos were based in Forty Projects, right around the corner from the block.

Cat considered Pap to be the ideal lieutenant because he was a man of his word and wasn't afraid to handle business. Pappy kept his operations in check, but more importantly he handled all Cat's problems, when they arose, as if they were his own. Pappy truly was his brother's keeper.

"When you think of Pap you think of an enforcer for Cat." BC says. "He had his own identity as far as getting busy. But to Cat he was a loyal, faithful soldier." Despite this discipline, Pap was a wild dude. He didn't give a fuck. He was blatant when it came to violence and although he followed Cat's orders precisely he did it with an overzealous abandonment. "Dude was lethal," D says. "That's the truth."

Pappy pistol whipped a prostitute who stole from Cat in broad daylight on the block, shot a rival dealer who tried to encroach on Cat's territory, and allegedly shot a customer dead outside a church, because the customer had the nerve to complain about the purity of Cat's product. These are some of the street legends that support Pappy's mythology.

"The people that label him legendary do so because he was a man of his word and if you were on his team and sometimes even if you weren't, he was with you 'til the end." D says. "You need a dude like that in your corner. You want him on your team." With Cat's best interests at heart, Pappy set a brutal precedent for the drug crew.

Fat Cat's workers regularly doused junkies who fell asleep on the block with gasoline and set them on fire. Dealers who skimmed money and drugs from the Cat were subject to varying degrees of torture, ten dollars would cost the offending dealers a beatdown. One hundred dollars meant a hot comb in the buttocks. Any theft over $1000 meant death. "Don't dis' me," Cat was heard to say. "Dis' me and you're dead."

Cat relied on his family for business purposes, but for serious acts of violence, he used Pappy. Pappy had no problem helping the Cat and was down for whatever Fat Cat had in mind. Pappy thrived on violence and possessed an almost visceral hatred of law enforcement. Pappy was the guy who was perpetually up for a fight, even with the cops.

"Cat liked to use guys from Brooklyn because it created a big element of surprise for the guys in Queens." A dude from the era said. "Everybody knew everybody in our neighborhood, so when these outsiders came in, it just threw everybody off." And with Queens off balance, Fat Cat took over.

CHAPTER 3
Blowing Up

**Cops began investigating the man they called the most
powerful dealer in the area, Fat Cat.**
***New York* Magazine.**

By 1985 Cat's transformation from small-time hoodlum,
to arguably the biggest name of his era in New York's black
underworld, was complete. Cat moved around South Jamaica
virtually untouched. He would have the occasional riff with the
dudes from Forty Projects and had no problems discipling his
crew or workers, but for the most part he was about fun and
money.

Sixty or so thousand a week was an average week, just off
dope. Heroin was the Cat's main source of income at the start.
Coke was moving, but crack wasn't around yet. Cat worked his
way up from a strong arm to kingpin, with a rep for cunning
strategic moves and brutal intimidation tactics. He was well-
known on the hard scrable streets and was often seen driving
flashy cars and wearing expensive jewelry.

"He was a role model for a lot of kids," D says. "When you
see a guy like that, with the clothes and the cars and everything,
you go, 'That's what I want to be when I grow up.'" It wasn't a

problem for Cat to be known as the man. He was the epitome of the new era black gangster.

Cat was wearing stuff the rappers sport now in 1985. He was living the lifestyle of the rich and infamous. A ghetto celebrity, whose every move created outward ripples. He was a grand chess master who rode around in Benz's, Porsche's and more. Always three steps ahead of the game, allowing him to indulge in whatever he wanted to. It was his God given right as far as he was concerned. As the biggest drug lord with the most gun thugs, no one challenged the Cat.

Money, power and respect combined to become the currency of his stature and position. In the hood he was a model of success. Cat and the other dealers in Queens were icons. "Everybody wanted to be like him. He had the money, the cars, the women." Ethan Brown said. "Fat Cat was the biggest drug dealer in Queens."

Rap was taking hold in Queens at the same time Cat was making his mark in the streets. Russell Simmons was in effect and doing the hip-hop thing. Promoting and pushing the music, culture and artists. Cat and the other drug dealers were big supporters of the burgeoning scene. The flash in hip-hop would come to emulate the indulgences of the gangsters. Their fashions inspired the entertainers and set the trends.

"In the 80s many hustlers in the streets of New York had more money, cars, jewelry and women than the dudes that were rapping and singing," Dex says. "We had the VIP in clubs and was popping all the bottles. All one had to do was go to clubs like The Fever in the Bronx, or The Roxy, Harlem World, Red Parrot, Broadway International, Funhouse in Manhattan to know who was running shit. What I'm saying is these entertainers wanted to be like us."

Run DMC would rep the Adidas, fat chains and leather suits. Their music epitomized the gangster b-boy style that dudes in the hood invented. But Run DMC brought that Queens b-boy style to the masses. With the advent of the music video and the explosion of hip-hop, the flavor of the streets of Queens reverberated nationwide. At clubs, shows and in magazines the culture was celebrated.

"There was a definite influence as Queens drug dealers mingled with the up-and-coming hip-hop stars." D says. "The drug dealers were who the rappers wanted to be. They emulated their style." It was a juxtaposition of swagger, attitude and outlook. "Back in the day hip-hop was trying to be like us," Shocker says. In the streets the drug lords represented everything that was cool and hip.

Cat rubbed elbows with Run DMC and LL Cool J. He knew Russell Simmons. They were in his circle, but back then Cat and his crew were the stars. The hip-hoppers were only curiosities. Just some kids on the block busting rhymes. The lives that Cat and his crew were living, were the dreams that the rappers were chasing. Their emulation came across in their art and music.

"We were the original hoodstars," Luc Spoon said. "One Christmas we had five white limos pick us up from the block and take us to Atlantic City for Cat's b-day. One limo was filled with cases of Dom Perigon and another with just chicks. We all chipped in and bought Cat a five-carat diamond pinky ring for his birthday that cost $100,000. We ran into Supreme and Prince. They had bagged two bad chicks, who ended up treating the whole crew like the superstars we were."

Once they arrived in Atlantic City, Cat bought the entire crew diamond encrusted gold medallions of their respective zodiac signs to show his thanks. "Life back then was like a non-stop party," D says. "The money spent was crazy It just didn't stop. No one thought it would end."

One of the crew's regular haunts was the Fontaineblue Hotel in Miami Beach. They also frequented the prize fights in Las Vegas and Atlantic City. Disco Fever in the Bronx, where DJ Starchild routinely saluted the crew by shouting "Queens in the house," was a routine hangout. Whenever Cat and company rolled in, they were on some *Entourage* type shit. All the reality shows nowadays got nothing on the crack era crews.

There were crazy parties happening all the time. The Olympic

Palace party has gone down in infamy. The photos have appeared in all the street magazines and shown the embarrassment of riches the hustlers adorned themselves with. That party was celebrated for Supreme and Wall Corley's birthdays, but Cat threw a party that topped that.

"The only party that took place back then that was bigger than that was Fat Cat's birthday." The dude from the era says. "It was in 84. Cat had the whole block surrounded with like 30 limousines and we rode from the block straight onto Atlantic City to one of Donald Trump's first hotels. Cat had like four whole floors on reserve. We had the Taj Mahal on lock. Cat had rooms with champagne from the floor to the ceiling. He had another room full of coke, at least 100 birds for everybody to enjoy themselves for free. I mean that shit was the craziest birthday party that I've ever been to."

It wasn't all partying; Cat had a serious side also. He opened his own deli on 150th Street and 107th Avenue that doubled as headquarters. He called it Big Mac's Deli. "Fat Cat's grocery store was the only one on the block that had no bars on the windows," a Queens narcotics cop said. Although Fat Cat kept no iron gates on his storefront, and assaults on rival drug dens were commonplace, no one ever made a move on Big Mac's Deli.

"They were too scared of Fat Cat and Pappy Mason to even think of doing such a thing." D says. The deli was known as "the game room" to locals and members of Cat's crew congregated there. "It was one of the few stores in the neighborhood that didn't have bars on the front or Plexiglas across the counter. Fear kept people out." D says. "That showed the influence Cat had."

Fat Cat's other business, the illicit enterprise, was well organized and lucrative. It consisted of heroin and powder cocaine. He hired his homeboys to run the spots. "Lorenzo presented opportunities for people that didn't have any options." Curtis Scoon said. "He controlled the block. His aura was that's that nigga for real."

At the height of his power he was said to have a crew of 30 associates helping with sales and enforcement. He controlled a large share of the areas 100 million a year drug trade. Fat Cat's strength was not in numbers, but in the people around him. Smart, devoted guys like Joseph "Bobo" Rodgers aka Mike Bones, Luc Spoon and Chris "Jughead" Williams. Their loyalty was unbreakable.

"We followed the old school street code. No rape, no stealing from each other, shit like that." Luc Spoon said. "My whole thing was to make sure whoever was with us ate. If we ate, you ate. I made sure everyone got paid. To avoid all the headaches, I'd make sure everybody from the bottom to the top got their proper change. I'd treat a dope fiend no different from a nigga getting money, if you right, you right. If you wrong, you wrong. That's how I carried it."

Fat Cat formed an alliance with the Corleys at Forty Projects, a large housing project near South Road in Jamaica, that undercover cops found virtually impenetrable. Cat figured with so much profit to be made, there was no sense in beefing over territory. He got with the Corleys and the other dealers in the area, including Claude Skinner, Kenneth "Supreme" McGriff, Gerald "Prince" Miller, Tommy "Montana" Mickens and Cornbread.

After a night of partying at the game room, the area was split up. The Supreme Team got Baisley Projects, the Corleys got Forty Projects and Tommy Montana got Lauralton and Hollis. Fat Cat kept the block. This collective was known as the Round Table and Cat headed it. "There was a spirit of cooperation in those days." D says. "They didn't sell to people they didn't know and they avoided getting the police involved."

As Cat gained power he began to distance himself from street sales and the violence that often occurred. "Fat Cat was like a legend. You never saw him." Shocker says. With half a dozen outlets in Queens, Brooklyn and Nassau County, Fat Cat's business was popping. He became the CEO of a drug empire that spanned the city.

"The main thing in the drug business is to insulate yourself," D says. "You have to have lower level people who are expendable if something goes wrong." Much of the responsibility for running the crew and enforcement was given to Pappy, Mike Bones, Luc Spoon and Jughead. They all played their position in the organization to perfection. "Pappy was the enforcer," Ethan Brown said. "He was the one who put in work."

Pappy had a vicious rep and Cat used that to his advantage. Street legend says Pappy stuck hot curling irons up dudes' asses to torture them or get them to talk. They said he was grimy and that he definitely did not play when it came to his or Cat's money. Pappy and the gun toting Bebos were a fearsome sight on the streets of Queens.

"That dude with the dreadlocks, that's Pappy. He's Fat Cat's enforcer now. He's the craziest dude out here." One informer told the police. Pappy and the Bebos had the whole hood shook. "He was a man's man. He was truly a gangster god. Never to be forgotten." Shocker says. The respect Pappy carried in the streets was iconic.

"Bebo is a way of life to Rastaman and Jah for real." Pappy said. "I am a man amongst men. I am Rasta for real. I am God's son." The Bebos had the hood on lockdown. "Those Bebo niggas they were out there. They had leather jackets with Bebo on it. They weren't worried about the police, because they knew the police wouldn't do nothing to them. They felt they was untouchable with the local police." BC says. "In my hood it was all Cat and Pap."

The dope game duo sent reverberations throughout Queens. Their run was as legendary as it was dramatic. Supreme from the Supreme Team even chimes in, "Pap was a real thorough dude." And Prince remembered when he met Pappy also. "The first person I met from Cat's crew when I came home from state prison on July 1, 1984 was Pap." Prince said.

With Pappy and the trigger happy Bebos, Cat's organization was at full strength. Nobody was trying to see them. They had the block and the spot at Forty Projects locked down. The Round Table was in effect, and Cat held all the cards. It was his world and he let everyone know it.

"Our projects name is South Jamaica Houses, but its better

known as Forty Projects," Shocker says. "Fat Cat and them were working out of the middle building I used to hang around. I was a gofer running errands. I would go the store for dudes. I met Pap first, but Cat knew my family. He knew my aunts. My grandma worked at the diner, so I always saw him because he knew my family, but I met Pap first.

"One day when I came home from school there was this light skinned dude with dreads. He asked me, 'Shorty you know where to get some sinsemilla?' He gave me some money and told me to get some weed, some Whiteout and some Guinness Stout. This was the first time I was ever near a Rasta." And this meeting proved pivotal in the young Shocker's life, thrusting him into the drug world and hip-hop lore.

"I go get everything and come back," Shocker says. "I give it to him and he rolls up the blunt. When he takes a pull I'm like 'Yo, dread, pass that shit.' He was like 'Sorry, shorty, I didn't know you smoke.' I was like 'Yo, my name is Shocker not shorty.' He was like 'Okay, I'm Ruff.' This was Pappy's brother from Brooklyn. Not his real brother, they just grew up together. He didn't know nobody in Queens. He was working security for Cat.

"We hit it off and hung out together everyday. I found out the spot belonged to Jughead. He comes by and Ruff and Jug are arguing. I'm holding Ruff's gun. Ruff tells Jug, 'I'm not your worker. I'm doing a favor for my brother.' Ruff tells Jug, 'You better step off or shorty will blast you,' meaning me. Jug rolls off. But the next day Ruff ain't there no more. He was like my best friend so I was fucked up." Shocker was a youngster, but he was eager to get into the game.

"I already decided I wanted to be a gangster, but after that situation I don't think I'm gonna be with Fat Cat," Shocker says. "Later on I'm in my project on 160th Street and I see this dude with dreadlocks on a pedal bike. The way he talked, his whole swag, he was like a gangster god." The dude on the bike was Pappy Mason.

"Three days later I seen Pap again. He's sitting on a car with a kid named Scotty. I was like 'Yo, Pap, what's up?'" Shocker says. "I don't even know him, but I know his brother. So I'm like 'What's up with Ruff?' Pap was like, 'He in Brooklyn, who are you?' I told him, 'I'm Shocker, Ruff's dude.' Pappy smiled then.

"Yeah, Ruff, him talk about you all the time.' I tell him to give me some weed. He gives me some money to buy it. I was on my high horse because I just talked to my idol." In the crack era Pappy had that affect on youngsters, but he also had work for those that were down.

"I saw Pap again and he told me he was opening up a spot on the 4th floor in my building and that Ruff would be back and that I could come up when Ruff came," Shocker says. "Ruff came back so I go up there with Ruff and I'm down. I got a walkie-talkie. One time the police run up, I get arrested, but I don't say anything, so I'm locked in with Pap for life.

"Almost everyone in my projects got down with Wall Corley. At one time Cat and Wall had a rivalry, but then worked it out and Cat started selling in the projects." With Pappy and by extension the Bebos, Cat expanded his reach. Solidifying his drug empire, as he became the boss of bosses. The Don Dada of the Southside of Jamaica, Queens.

"I'm an original Bebo." Shocker says. "Bebos came like 84 or 85. That's when we started calling each other Bebos. Most of us had dreads. They thought we were a Jamaican gang, but we weren't. There wasn't that many of us. It was a really good time in my life, cause I didn't have any brothers. It was like having a bunch of big brothers who would do whatever for me, who had my back against anybody and I had theirs too. We were all brothers from another mother and being a part of something.

"I was young, full of cum and having fun, but I didn't realize that I played a major part in the destruction of my people. There won't never be nobody like Pappy. He was a gangster god. He did a lot of good for people; he didn't like to see people get taken advantage of. He had an extremely big heart. He was like Robin Hood, the Prince of Thieves."

To his loyal soldiers Pappy was a benevolent leader but to the streets he was a whirlwind of terror. Under Cat he wreaked havoc in the hood. Pappy and the Bebos were given free reign as Cat and his organization held the streets hostage. From hand to hand hustler to drug baron, Fat Cat elevated the stakes of the drug game.

By the spring of 1985, Fat Cat's dealing had become more and more apparent to Brian Rooney, his parole officer. Rooney was mainly concerned with proof of employment, which Cat got easily from his future father-in-law, who on paper owned Big Mac's Deli. To his parole officer, Cat was a deli worker, but to the streets he was blowing up, riding around in European sports cars and wearing expensive jewelry.

"I just can't imagine anybody having that much money lying around," Rooney said. "Hell, he's got my yearly salary in a drawer." On paper, Fat Cat was working at the deli and as a carpenter for Imperial Home Improvements, a South Jamaica company owned by his wife Joanne McClinton, while living at home with his mother in a South Ozone Park house. But in reality Cat was rocketing to street stardom and enhancing his position in the drug world.

"Look," Rooney would tell his parolees. "If you do something wrong again, I'm going to put you in jail. I'm going to put you away." Cat was polite and diffident to his parole officer, but didn't really pay him any mind. He figured it was all just formalities. The Cat felt he had it all covered. He thought he was above the law.

"We didn't know what we were dealing with at the time," said Richard Levy, the Director of Parole. "The police knew and some of our own parolees knew that this was a major drug dealer, but we didn't. When we'd come around his workplace or home, people would cover for him saying he was out on an errand or something." And this lack of intel would end up proving tragic, as all the power and influence went to Cat's head.

CHAPTER 4
The Bust

I'm rich/I still wake up with crime on my mind/
Queens nigga/Put it down like Pappy Mason in his
prime. I Don't Need 'em, 50 Cent, The Massacre,
(2005)

By 1985, Fat Cat and Pappy were in their prime, career wise.
Cat had like thirty dudes under him and his organization was
growing, due to all the sub-organizations under him like the
Bebos and to an extent the Supreme Team. "Cat started all of
them." Shocker says, "He put them all on, the whole Round
Table, except Wall Corley. He put Preme on and then Preme
went on his own, just like Pap went on his own, but we were still
under Cat to an extent."

While Preme was doing his thing at Baisley Projects, Pap's
penchant was the enforcer who held down the crew. Everybody
played their position and Cat controlled it all at the head of the
Round Table. The puppet master behind the scenes, pulling all
the strings. He was subtle, only showing his hand when necessary.
Cat had stepped back from the streets and made himself less
visible. Like Don Corleone in *The Godfather* he was calling the
shots in secrecy.

Fat Cat's attempt to insulate himself from arrest failed completely in July of 1985. Queens Narcotics cops grabbed Stony Bastion, one of Cat's dealers, in a buy and bust operation. Stony had a long rap sheet that went back years for all types of petty crimes. As a repeat offender he was looking at jail time, knowing that Stony offered the only play he had.

"I can give you Fat Cat," Stony told the cops. He was registered as an informant and put back on the streets. A few weeks later, Stony walked to a payphone and called his handlers, "Hit the Cat's place, it's hot." The snitch had done his job and the police moved in, happily obliged to make the bust.

At 10 p.m. on July 29, 1985, twenty Queens cops hit Fat Cat's store, a search warrant in hand. To their amazement, the cops found Fat Cat, Jughead, Luc Spoon and Rita Maynor sitting in the store with drugs and money visible. One of Cat's cardinal rules was no drug dealing from inside any of his properties. Everyone adhered to this rule without exception, so it came as a shock when the cops from the 103rd Precinct busted into Nichols' private office at the deli with guns drawn, and found a pound of marijuana on Cat's desk.

"Motherfucker," Cat said. He was caught with his pants down and hands in the cookie jar. Fat Cat reached for the weapons in his desk drawer when the cops entered, but they had him covered. It was a tense moment. Would Cat make a move for his guns or not?

"He was sitting on two loaded automatic weapons and had a .9 mm eighteen shot automatic in his drawer when we came in," one of the cops said. "He seemed to make a move for them, but then he realized that wasn't such a good idea as I had him covered." The cops were uneasy for a few seconds. They knew if Fat Cat pulled the guns it would get messy. A moment of uncertainty caused trigger fingers to tighten.

One of the weapons was a Steyr assault rifle. It was one of the most lethal weapons in the world. If Fat Cat wanted he could have blasted his way out of the deli. He could have gone out in a hail of bullets, adding to his legend in the annals of gangster lore.

Fat Cat must have known he was hit.

The deli was loaded with drugs and cash. The combination of cash, drugs and guns meant Fat Cat would likely face a long prison sentence, perhaps 25-to-life, under the harsh Rockefeller drug laws. It wasn't a winning proposition. Better to hold court in the streets and be carried by six, then judged by twelve at the government's mercy.

"Fat Cat reached for the Steyr," the cop said, "because he knew his time was up." But Fat Cat didn't pull the trigger, for whatever reason, he thought better and surrendered. It was a humiliating day for Queens foremost drug lord. When it came to the moment of truth Cat's gangster faltered, a sign of things to come.

"They nailed him at his mother's grocery store with 200 grand cash and weapons," D says. "The cops also found six ounces of high-grade heroin, two ounces of coke, ten pounds of marijuana, a money counting machine, a scale and a police radio scanner tuned to police broadcasts."

The police also found a card pinned to the wall. This was what Fat Cat looked at as he put down the Steyr. The card was inscribed, "World's Greatest Daddy" and was signed by one of Fat Cat's three children. As he contemplated going out like a gangster, the thought of his children made him reconsider. Call it what you want, but that moment of clarity just showed that the Cat was human after all.

"That take down was a big hit, he was arrested with 200k cash and packaged drugs with a street value of 500 grand," Ethan Brown said. "That was the beginning of the end for Fat Cat. He kept the streets supplied with dope. But he didn't know when to stop. He had so much power, it was incredible."

Outside the deli, a huge biased crowd had gathered on the sidewalk. Word of the bust tore through the streets and those who didn't get word of the bust could tell something big was happening from the mass of cop cars parked outside, sirens blaring. The cops marched Cat, Jughead, Spoon and Rita out of the deli in handcuffs.

As Cat was being escorted to a police car by the arresting officer, Pappy Mason slipped behind the cop and was prepared to shoot him point blank in the head, to free Cat. But Fat Cat shook his head and mouthed the word, "No" to his enforcer, so Pappy put his gun away and disappeared into the crowd as Cat was put in the police car and taken away.

"Before we were even done with the search his lawyer showed up." The cop said. "The strange thing was Nichols had not even made a phone call." Fat Cat's guns and drugs attorney, David Cohen, arrived on the scene before police drove his client away. "We'd never seen anything like that before," the cop later told *Newsday* and *New York* magazine. Police took the Cat and his cohorts to Queensboro Correctional facility.

"They put Fat Cat in a separate cell from the rest of us and cops and detectives from all over the city came to get a look at him. It was like they wanted to show off their prize catch." Luc Spoon said. The whole crew was released the next day on cash bonds, Cat's was 70 grand. "I don't think they really understood how much money I was making until then." Fat Cat said.

As far as the wheels of justice were concerned, it didn't matter how much money the Cat was making. By getting arrested he had violated the terms of his probation. Two weeks later when Cat showed up for a 4 p.m. meeting with his parole officer he was put in handcuffs once more. "You're going right back in," Brian Rooney told Fat Cat as he grabbed his gun and escorted the Cat to the local lock up.

"Brian mentioned that this guy was a major drug dealer with a dangerous reputation so we had to be careful," a fellow parole officer said. At the subsequent parole hearing, Rooney advised the court that he suspected Lorenzo Nichols of being a drug kingpin and vicious gangster. It didn't look good for the Cat, he was digging himself into a deeper and deeper hole without even trying. This left him defiant to the extreme.

In August 1985, the Cat was returned to prison. He was furious and his anger would have harrowing consequences. "What did the crazy fuck expect me to do?" Rooney asked his coworker. "If I don't have the balls to do my job what good am I?" But Rooney's decision to lock the Cat back up would prove fatal.

The violation left the boss in jail and with the Cat indisposed; Pappy's importance in the organization grew. He became the defacto shotcaller for the area. Not only was he running his own crew, but he was in charge of security and was the number one man for the whole Fat Cat organization.

Pappy Mason began to make regular visits to the Queens House of Detention in September 1985 to receive instructions from his boss. Sometimes Pappy brought along Jughead and Perry Bellamy. Cat relayed his orders through them. The prospect of spending life in prison had not done much for Cat's disposition. He was still in charge; he just moved his office to the jail.

Like any good boss, the Cat wouldn't let something small like prison deter him, he was still running his drug empire. He would not cede control to anyone. Fat Cat kept business humming at Big Mac's Deli, issuing directives from his prison cell and entrusting higher ups like Pappy, Luc Spoon, Mike Bones and Jughead to execute them on the streets.

Under Cat's careful guidance, the Nichols organization was becoming the rare crew to deal in weight and retail quantities of drugs. The crew's profits reflected the whole spectrum of the business. They were generating millions of dollars in cash. The Cat's organization was both powerful and profitable, thanks to a wide ranging network of sub-organizations like the Bebos and his other trusted lieutenant's crews.

It didn't matter if the boss was in jail; Cat had it set up like the Mafia. He had the reins of power and he refused to relinquish them. When shit jumped off in the hood, Southeast Queens residents could often be heard remarking, "Cat's letting out the wolves again." He was the king and heavy was the head that wore the crown.

As Fat Cat sat in prison awaiting trial in the fall of 1985, his crew plotted revenge. During a phone call from prison Fat Cat instructed Pappy, Jughead and Mike Bones to hire a hitman to seriously injure his parole officer Brian Rooney. Because prison phones were monitored the Cat was purposely vague in giving the order.

"Listen up, homes," Nichols told them. "You motherfuckers better take care of Busy's problem. Man, fuck that parole officer. P.O. or on P.O., he's going to get what's coming to him." Jughead and Pappy put the plan into motion. But even the best laid plans go astray.

On the evening of October 9, 1985, Jughead went to Pappy's girlfriend's house to receive a telephone call from the Cat. The imprisoned drug dealer and Jughead talked for about half an hour. Later Jughead cornered Perry Bellamy, one of Cat's underlings and let him know what was going down outside the A & B Cabstand on Baisley Boulevard.

"Yo, man," Jughead said. "I want you to do something for me. I want you to bring Cat's P.O. to the park." When Perry asked why, Jughead told him. "Don't worry about it. I'm going to call him tomorrow. You just meet me at the game room at 11:30 a.m." The Cat was power mad, and his imprisonment left him in a frenzy. Someone would pay, he decided. It was vital for him to show the world that no one crossed the Cat.

In the morning, Jughead and Perry met near a pay phone outside a McDonald's on Sutphin Boulevard. Jughead telephoned Brian Rooney and told the parole officer he had some information on Fat Cat. Rooney was told to meet Perry at 7 p.m. on Sutphin Boulevard. Jughead was orchestrating the move and giving the orders, but Pappy Mason carried the gun, his partner Ruff was armed also.

Rooney pulled his 1974 Dodge Dart up to the corner of 119th Avenue and 155th Street in South Jamaica and Perry flagged him down and got in the car. As Perry talked excitedly to Rooney, Ruff came up out of the bushes and fired one shot, hitting the passenger door frame. "Jesus Christ," Rooney screamed and tried to restart his car. But it was too late.

Just as the engine turned over Pappy stepped to his window and fired a large black .9 mm into the car. Pappy fired twice, hitting Rooney in the chest and a second time in the left arm. The car lurched forward and Pappy reached to open the door. "Get the fuck out of the car," Pappy yelled to Perry, who looked stunned. When the cops were called to the scene of what they believed would be a routine car accident, they found Rooney slumped over the wheel, dead. This murder was the beginning of the end for Fat Cat and the Southside of Jamaica drug crews. They just didn't know it yet.

"Brian Rooney was shot dead at a traffic stop. It was a surprise." Ethan Brown said. At the time, Rooney's death seemed like little more than a random street murder in one of the most unforgiving parts of Queens. "Right now the motive for the murder is a mystery," a cop admitted just after the shooting. But it would all come out.

After the hit, Pappy was deciding on whether to kill Perry Bellamy. He wasn't sure Bellamy could be trusted to keep his mouth shut. Pappy was against leaving around any perceived weak links; he would rather deal with them and be finished with it, once and for all. The assassins resurfaced at Jack's Grocery store on the corner of 150th Street and Liberty Avenue. Perry exited the car and Pappy grabbed him.

"If I hear you even say one fucking thing about this, I will kill you." Pappy said. "If I can't get you, I will get your family. Shit, I should fucking do you right here." Pappy began laughing with Ruff and Jughead. He told them, "We lose one of ours. They lose one of theirs. We got to show that Busy still got the juice."

The killing had the opposite effect. It was a critical error of judgment that would hasten Cat and Pappy's demise. It was one thing to shoot and kill other dealers and denizens of the block, but to have the audacity to kill a law enforcement figure, that was crazy.

"The parole officer got murdered in October. Two weeks later Perry Bellamy gets arrested and indicates Cat had it done and points to Pappy as the shooter. He told the cops he was used to lure the parole officer there." Luc Spoon said. Weak links always snitch, it's inevitable.

Bellamy told homicide detective David Dellnegro that he was willing to talk about the killing. Dellnegro called assistant Queens District Attorney Joseph Keenan and by midnight Perry Bellamy was sitting in the office of the District Attorney's Homicide Bureau making a videotaped confession. He told the story in thirty seven minutes, implicating Pappy, Jughead, Ruff and Fat Cat in the assassination.

"They was all there when the P.O. got killed," Bellamy told the District Attorney. "Pappy he just open fire. Pappy got him. That shit was swift." Bellamy also told them that Fat Cat said, "Do that nigga, Perry. I want the P.O. popped." Fat Cat was on some Pablo Escobar type time, but that *Scarface* mentality would backfire on him.

The Rooney hit would set off a chain of targeted assassinations on the streets that would last more than a decade. Nobody could foresee the carnage that would ensue. Bodies would drop and turf wars would escalate. The street legends of Queens would rise in infamy and murder in a maelstrom of violence.

"The cops were shocked that Fat Cat ordered the P.O.'s death." Ethan Brown said. It was a tragic event that caught the police unprepared and left law enforcement scrambling. In Queens, the rising level of violence left the residents terrified of the young drug lords. Their brutalness was ready and evident. The community was under siege.

Pappy had serious juice on the street and his cold-blooded antics put fear into people's hearts. "He was a motherfucking killer. His influence was strong. He had a big influence," BC says. "Wasn't nobody trying to cross Cat or Pappy after that at all. Kill a P.O.? That shit was crazy."

Another informant surfaced, giving police some crucial information for their files. "I'm out on the street eighteen to twenty hours a day. I steal and I sell to everybody on the street," the informant told police. "I know Cat. I know the Corleys. I know Supreme. I know Prince and I know Skinner. I do work for them."

What he meant was that he delivered packages for them. The

informant was a gold mine for police. He was used by Skinner, Fat Cat and the Corleys to drop off packages. The cops sat him down and started going through all the homicide folders. He had information on everything and everybody. He connected all the dots.

He came back the next day and started making out a chart for the police. He told police about a guy named Cornbread and a guy named Hymie. He drew the whole drug hierarchy out for the police, giving them the A to Z, including Fat Cat's whole organization right down to the sleepers.

He was even talking about the Rooney murder. With the new informant, Billy Martin, and Perry Bellamy's videotaped implication, the police had all the evidence they needed to indict the Cat and Pappy for the murder. But they didn't act fast enough. In the swirl of chaos more drama erupted.

Fat Cat's favorite girlfriend, Myrtle "Misha" Horsheim, who was carrying Cat's son at the time, got arrested on a narcotics possession charge in New Jersey. She wrote a threatening note to Fat Cat, signing the letter Mrs. Busy. The letter included the phrase, "What goes around, comes around."

Fat Cat took this to mean she was going to give him up on the Rooney murder. He put his pit bull Pappy on her. "I don't know what you know," Pappy warned Misha. "But Busy says you sure better forget it." There were other loose ends that Cat needed tied up. He wasn't taking any chances with his freedom. In the face of adversity the Cat became the ultimate chess player, moving pieces to minimize the damage the defectors were causing him.

Word hit the street that Stony Bastion had been the one who rolled over on Cat. Pappy figured that Stony had traded his own freedom for Cats. That same October, as Stony was walking down 150th Street, Pappy approached him from behind. "I want to talk to you," Pappy told him and Stony started to run.

That was all the confession Pappy needed. He pulled out a .9 mm and fired. "That's one for Cat," Pappy said as Stony died on the sidewalk. Bellamy was next on Pappy's hit list, but he couldn't find him. When police went looking for Pappy though, he was easier to find.

In February 1986, Queens Detectives arrested Pappy for the murder of the P.O. on Bellamy's statement. Pappy was caught off guard, he had a loaded .22 caliber Derringer in his boot he was trying to get to, when the cops ran down on him and arrested him. Asked to cooperate in the affair and implicate Fat Cat, his boss, Pappy told police, "I ain't no Perry Bellamy." Because of his refusal to break the street code and uphold his death before dishonor ideal, Pappy joined his boss in the Queens House of Detention. "They got Cat in 85. Pap in 86. Pap went in right after Cat." D says. "Cat got arrested for being caught in the store with drugs. Pap got arrested for the P.O."

CHAPTER 5
The Man

Fat Cat and the Crack Wars, Brash Young Dealers Muscle the Drug Establishment, New York magazine.

Even after the parole violation that sent him to prison, and the incarceration of his enforcer Pappy Mason, Cat ran his organization on the streets and wielded tremendous influence. "Cat had the utmost respect from major dudes that would move out for him in a second. No doubt," BC says. "His name was ringing all over the city. His influence was so strong. The homie kept it poppin' without question. His trusted people were Mike Bones, the Fuertado Brothers and others, they moved for him while he was on the inside." Cat's control even from his prison cell was absolute.

"Fat Cat was a drug dealer, gangster, ghetto entrepreneur. He was the biggest name in his time in the 80s," Curtis Scoon said. "He owned deli's, laundry mats, home improvement companies. He had property in New York, Virginia, Alabama. He liked to live the best he could. Swimming pools in every house." His family enjoyed the fruits of his labor, Cat made sure of that.

Cat reaped the rewards of the dope game, even when he was in prison. His stature as a money maker never changed. But while he was away his organization's reputation for violence grew. "I kept the peace when I was on the streets, but with me gone, they had to show everyone they could answer the call," Cat said. With the Cat away the mice would play.

"When you are running a million dollar organization and you're not there, you have other people that want to think for you," Luc Spoon said. "When you're there you got different people thinking different things. You can't control that, because it's just too many people. You may control your inner circle and so on. Its just too many people that's left to do what they feel they want to do. But as in all business, if you're the leader you're gonna get the blame no matter what. When shit happens, Cat's gonna get the blame."

Cat loved the power he had, although he probably regretted the consequences that responsibility incurred. Because when it all crumbled, the authorities held Cat responsible. That was the price he would pay for wearing the crown. A fair trade off at the time. As the king of the drug thugs his influence was tremendous and given the fact he was in jail, it was remarkable that he kept the reins of power.

Cat was not only running his own crew, he was at the top of the pyramid over other crews too. The informant confirmed this with police. "He stated that the Nichols family is at the top of the drug trade. He believes Fat Cat's mother and his sister are running the drug operation while Fat Cat is in jail. Mort (Cat's sister) definitely supplies drugs and is always accompanied by an unknown male Oriental." The narcotics cop said.

"The following families are supplied by the Nichols family: Earlie Tripp, Abdula, Mustafa, Bebos and the Supreme Team. Skinner is on a level just under Fat Cat and operates independent of Fat Cat. Earlie Tripp operates in the area of 150th Street and 107th Avenue. Kandu, Stanly and Boom work for Earl. Abdula aka Unk sells from the game room at 106-56 150th Street. Re, Fats and Man work for him. Mustafa's crew is run by Bugout and Saleem, Cee, Hines and Unique work their territory on Inwood Street. The Bebos are Pappy's crew. They are run by Marshal.

That's Pappy's boy. He's like the sheriff out here. I seen him with Divine, Scott, Shocker. Call themselves the Bebos." All these crews were under Cat according to the informant.

"His presence in my hood was monstrous without question." BC says. "A lot of people speak about Preme and Prince, but you rarely heard about them in my hood, everything was Cat and it just wasn't on my block, Lakewood and Inwood, but it expanded from the block (150th-107th) through Sutphin and Rockaway. From 127th and 11th Avenue to Linden and the Van Wyck, from Rockaway and the Van Wyck to Liberty and Sutphin and everything in between. Inwood and South Road to 11th Avenue and 160th." Even in prison the Cat was a major player, but crack would change all that.

At the height of New York's crack era, Fat Cat reached Son of Sam status, dominating headlines and becoming the stuff of local lore. Despite being incarcerated throughout much of his reign, Fat Cat, with the acumen of a business maverick and the command of an ancient warlord, ruled what was then the largest street level drug ring in the Big Apple. But post crack, it would be a different story.

In the mid-80s, the crack vial spawned violence and bloodshed, paper chasers and four corner hustlers, drug empires and kingpins galore. The drug's climax would prove earth shattering. Crack changed Queens. It changed the way the dope game was played. Prior to the explosion, Queens had known violence, but not to the degree it would. Crack was a game changer.

"Crack comes out full scale. It came out a little bit right before we came in, but by the time, say 90 days after, it was rapid. Like once they closed 150th Street after our arrest, now you got offshots shooting up all over the place and it's not organized, its just niggas doing they thing, they just out there now. Every corner is a drug area with a lot of money floating around, because you had like a million or two coming through the area." Luc Spoon said.

One afternoon in November, 1985, Fat Cat was sitting in the

prison day room and called his sister Viola. "Hey Busy," she said. "That new stuff, people is wild for it." Cat didn't know what she was talking about. "What stuff is that?" He asked. "The stuff they be calling crack. It comes in a vial. And the homeboys is going crazy for it." Viola answered. Crack was about to put New York in a chokehold, UFC style.

"When crack first hit it was crazy bananas," Shocker says. "Before crack there were some crews getting money, but when crack hit the scene all these broke ass-motherfuckers started getting rich. Crack is a poor man's drug. It's not like heroin. I've seen mothers literally selling their baby's soul for a hit off the pipe. The invention of crack was a curse and a gift to the game."

At first, Cat didn't want to get into crack. He was already making crazy money. "Biz never wanted to sell crack," D says. "He thought it brought too much heat to the business." Fat Cat's lieutenant Mike Bones agreed with his boss's assessment. "We didn't need crack," Mike Bones said. "We was making crack money way before there was ever crack. Some weeks, we even had a million in cash."

Crack was a Godsend for the low-level, hand-to-hand dealers grinding on the block. Suddenly an individual hustler could pull in thousands of dollars a day. If he was willing to grind, the money was there. Newcomers could share in a business that had long been inaccessible, thanks to the monopolistic policies of established crews like Fat Cat's and the Supreme Team.

"There was a time when you wanted to be involved in crime you were selected by older guys." Curtis Scoon said. "With crack it just put everybody out there." This in turn meant that the streets were swarmed with naive, inexperienced hustlers. "The privates had become generals," Luc Spoon said. "You had guys on the streets who had only experienced the drugs and the easy cash, but had never faced any consequences for their behavior."

Crack started with the Dominicans, who were the retailers between the street guys and the Colombian suppliers. They were very smart marketers and crack soon replaced powdered cocaine as the drug of choice. Eventually Fat Cat had to give in and start selling crack. He couldn't afford not to sell it. With all his customers coming through requesting it, Cat's crew started supplying it.

By 1986, the crack trade in Queens was being called a $100 million a year industry. Following up on his sister's information, Fat Cat became the King of Crack. The imprisoned dealer's mother, sisters and brothers were running the business in his absence, while Pappy Mason recruited enforcers amongst the prison population and sent them out to handle the crew's business.

A crack dealer, prison officials determined, earned prestige on both sides of the prison wall. Just as gun thugs were attracted to the Mafia guys in prison, now they were all on Fat Cat's nuts. At the end of the day it was all about money and Fat Cat and Pappy Mason held the keys to the bank vault.

One of the gun thugs Pappy recruited to work for Cat was Brian "Glaze" Gibbs. He was an A-Team associate before he became an enforcer for Cat. The A-Team was a ruthless and feared crew from East New York's Cypress Projects that had no respect for the law and were known to rob drug dealers. Glaze got down with the A-Team at a young age and helped run the Dominicans off Fountain Avenue. They ran their drug business twenty-four/seven and made 10 grand a day and 20 grand on weekends.

"I met Pappy during the time of the parole officer murder and we became cool in prison," Glaze said. "I loved and respected Fat Cat. I made sure all the workers had enough work and I delegated the plans when Fat Cat said someone had to be killed. First time I shot someone I was 16-years-old, but the first time I killed someone I was 21-years-old. It was just another job for me and it was a part of me and I accepted my responsibility." Pappy and Cat sent killers out from prison to enforce their will.

The promising, but perilous state of Fat Cat's organization was mirrored by the powerful new drug. Crack fattened the bottom lines of the drug organizations, but also created a new set of problems. From rampant drug addiction to low-level hustlers suddenly being thrust into the position of street bosses. Even Fat Cat, always fearless in the toughest of situations, was worrying about the future.

One particular concern was the increasing number of women engaging in high-risk activity in his crew, like his sister Viola. Viola did whatever she could to help Fat Cat with the family business. She was gung-ho in accomplishing whatever needed to be done. "Her phone served as a switchboard for Cat," assistant U.S. Attorney Leslie Caldwell said. "There were some pretty blatant conversations. Viola was very talkative."

Fat Cat knew that women caught by the cops were much more likely than men to cooperate with law enforcement in return for reduced sentences. Even from behind bars, Fat Cat exerted tremendous control over his organization, but there was little he could do to prevent his relatives from participating in the riskiest aspects of the family business. They wanted to carry their weight and Cat trusted them.

With the astonishing ascent of the Nichols organization, each of its players, from the lowest bagger to the most feared lieutenant, now faced the fate of the imprisoned CEO. Fat Cat had become more powerful in prison than he ever was on the streets, but instead of being a blessing, this was a curse. Everything he loved was involved in his drug business.

"I seen him make a million dollars a week," D says. "He had so much power, his word was law. He made a crew member shoot himself in the leg while he was on the phone, because the guy didn't do what he was told about placing a large wager on a fight." This incident has passed into gangster lore and has been retold so many times it seems like a scene out of a movie.

Fat Cat told one of his henchmen to bet 50 g's on Sugar Ray Leonard before the Hagler/Sugar Ray fight in 1987. Sugar Ray was a three to one underdog after a three year self-imposed retirement. No one thought Sugar Ray would win, but the Cat had a hunch. The henchman failed to place the bet. Four nights later, four of Cat's lieutenants met in a Queens basement, awaiting a call from their imprisoned boss.

As the minutes passed, they shifted anxiously in their seats, tension thick in the air. The call came in. The penalty – shoot yourself or be shot, was equal parts kind and savage. The lieutenant opted for the former and was handed a Browning semi-automatic .9 mm. It was do or die time.

With the phone line still open he cocked the gun and fired a single shot into his thigh. He winced in pain bleeding and yelling expletives, yet proud to have taken his punishment. Gun still in hand the man grabbed the phone to confirm Cat's satisfaction. Upon approval he hung up the phone and raced to Mary Immaculate Hospital. The Cat was pleased in his jail cell, but life in the ghetto went on.

As hustlers got money and the community descended into chaos, residents openly spoke on how crack trafficking became a plague in their once peaceful neighborhood. Mothers, fathers, sisters, brothers, sons and daughters- no one was immune to the lure of crack. As the epidemic spun out of control, law enforcement tried to win back the streets. But it was a losing cause.

Investigators had been trying to build cases against Fat Cat for drug dealing and the P.O. murder. It was difficult to get people to say much about Nichols, and the denizens of the block were absolutely terrified of Pappy Mason. It was well-known in the streets that informants and cooperators were routinely killed. "There's not a single soul who is gonna testify against that boy." A local resident said. The fear generated by the drug lords was palpable. People were scared before, but crack ratcheted up the violence to new levels. The burgeoning violence was erupting like a volcano and Pappy Mason was at the center of it.

"He was a big presence in Queens," BC says. "He was a wild nigga." Like the Cat before him, Pappy's incarceration only increased his powers. Between the two street gangsters, they emitted a brazen killing aura of menace and power. Whatever words they uttered were law. No questions asked. No quarter given. The South Jamaica streets were boiling with fury and malice, the crack vial being at the epicenter of all the action and reaction.

In 1987, Fat Cat was finally arraigned in State Supreme Court in Queens on second degree murder charges for arranging the murder of Brian Rooney. Pappy Mason was also indicted. Perry Bellamy pled guilty and was convicted of setting up the murder. He was sentenced to 25-to-life, even though he turned rat. Despite the time lapse, the authorities were determined to convict the responsible parties.

"Lorenzo Nichols was a suspect almost from the beginning," Queens District Attorney John Santucci said. "Not only did the slaying take place in his territory, but he was the most likely candidate because of his sensitivity to the parole violation that Rooney nailed him for." Cat's bail was raised to two million.

"At first we were afraid Nichols would be able to afford that too, but I guess after all that time in jail, his resources were a little depleted." Santucci said. But Cat was playing the waiting game. Trying to find loopholes in the law to beat the case. He was fighting two cases, but he was confident he could connive his way out of the legal mess he found himself in. It didn't look good though, as the District Attorney's office appeared to have a tight case.

"Their motive was revenge, because Brian Rooney had put him back behind bars," a prosecutor told Justice Thomas Demaleos. Pappy, Ruff and Perry Bellamy "were only agents, contract killers acting at the orders of this defendant. Lorenzo Nichols was behind the murder." The District Attorney's office was going full tilt in their effort for a conviction.

Fat Cat stood silently behind the bench as his popular guns-and-drugs lawyer, David Cohen, told the court, "The plea is not guilty. This is one of the flimsiest and weakest cases to ever come before your honor. If they had concrete and physical evidence, my client would have been indicted two years ago." He contended that Fat Cat, "had no motive" to kill the parole officer, because the defendant knew that the decision to return him to prison was not just up to Rooney.

Fat Cat waved to his mother, Louise Coleman and to several

other people in the spectator section as he was escorted from the courtroom after the arraignment. Outside the court, Ms. Coleman said concerning the charge that her son masterminded the parole officer's murder, "He didn't do it. I'll put my neck on the chopping block that he didn't do it."

The prosecutor didn't talk about Fat Cat's alleged drug empire, but the state was building a case against the Cat for dealing drugs also. Both cases were taking a long time to bring to trial. The state was having a hard time finding witnesses, they kept getting killed.

In December 1987, after discovery was granted in the second degree murder case, Fat Cat silenced his talkative girlfriend Myrtle "Misha" Horsheim. Pappy had told her to be quiet, but she didn't listen. Cat must have thought he could kill all the witnesses. They were disappearing at an alarming rate, so it definitely seemed he was trying.

"Cat said he had his son's mother killed because he felt disrespected by her when he was in prison." A convict who knew Fat Cat says. While driving through the Forty Projects with a girlfriend in a blue Monte Carlo, Misha noticed a black car following her. The chase car, a black Volvo with tinted windows and gold trim wheels, cornered her at the end of a one way street. She was trapped.

Two men, one carrying a .9 mm, the other with a .380 semi-automatic, got out of the car. One of the men reached in and took Fat Cat's eighteen-month-old son out of the car. The man placed the baby on the sidewalk and then turned back to the car. Both men opened fire. Misha was killed instantly. Fat Cat's son was later found wandering the streets. Misha's girlfriend recovered, but never felt inclined to identify her attackers.

"Fat Cat gave me the order and I killed her," Glaze said. "There was a lot of rumors, but the real reason is because Cat was getting nervous about her loyalty so he wanted her dead. She did a lot of fucked up shit. She would say her house was robbed for the drugs that Cat left at her house and he didn't believe her. I was in charge of what I liked to do and that was murder. I took the murder game real serious. Fat Cat taught me to always keep my hands clean by placing people in the middle of me, but I chose to do a lot of my murders myself."

Cat had more debts to settle from his prison cell. On trial for the Rooney murder, he was trying to kill all who crossed him. Two stick-up kids, cousins Issac and Henry Boldin were shot for a robbery on one of Cat's stash houses. With the Cat away, the canaries tried to play, but when Cat caught wind of the robbery, he sent the order out to murder the cousins.

One was killed, but the other survived. It wasn't clean like Cat wanted, but the murder served its purpose. The robbery and other setbacks screamed weakness to the streets and Cat had to reassert his power before other stick-up kids pounced like vultures. The Cat's prolonged absence and decline in respect left a void, instead of being untouchable, he had finally become a target.

The Cat's wife of ten years, Joanne "Mouse" Nichols lived in an expensive Elmont, Long Island home, far from South Jamaica's killing fields. One Friday as she was driving from a store, back to her split-level home, in a black 1985 Mercedes Benz, she was forced to the side of the road by another car. The men said they were cops and produced a subpoena with her name on it.

They said they were investigating Mouse in connection with the Rooney murder. She was handcuffed and placed in a blue car. She was then blindfolded and put in a van which took her to an apartment in Brooklyn. Over 18 hours, the kidnappers made repeated phone calls to her mother on Long Island and her in-laws in South Ozone Park, demanding twenty-two pounds of cocaine and 50 grand in cash for her release.

"The kidnappers threatened me with pit bulls," Mouse said. "They said they were going to let the dogs bite my breast off." At first family members couldn't come up with the money and the police were contacted. But over the weekend Cat called home and the family quickly came up with 77 grand in cash. Early Sunday morning, the money was dropped off in a garbage can outside a Brooklyn White Castle and Joanne Nichols returned home in a taxi. "The kidnappers thought her family, specifically her husband, was involved in drugs." Fred Klein, a Nassau County assistant District Attorney said. "They seem like real amateurs only asking for 77 grand from Fat Cat. I think he could have afforded a lot more than that."

But the perpetrators didn't get away with it. Four men were eventually arrested and convicted at trial. At the trial, Mouse testified that she had received a dead mouse in the mail before taking the stand. The envelope also included three bullets. Each bullet Mouse reported had been inscribed with one of her children's names. It later turned out that the same men had also abducted and killed another of the Cat's workers. The men did not appear very frightened of the Cat.

With the drug induced body count in Queens rising, and the murders of ordinary people for testifying or complaining, the Cat had many enemies. People attached his name to anything that happened. Cat became the one to blame for all the community's evils. And with him and Pappy in prison his power was waning.

"Fat Cat has been trying to do his thing from inside the can, but he's like a wounded lion now and the jackals are nipping at his heels." A cop said. "After what's happened this summer, it's clear that Fat Cat no longer has absolute control. The young guys have no respect for him. A lot of the young crack guys out there will shoot anybody who gets in their way and they don't worry about the consequences.

"They make Fat Cat look mature. If Fat Cat was out no one would pull anything like this. We knew if Fat Cat got out either he'd be in the wind or bodies would fall in Queens. These drug guys are absolutely nuts. They're way worse than the Mafia. They're so young and so violent that they don't have the restraint that the more traditional organized crime guys have."

Fat Cat's organization was cratering. As the charges piled up against the Cat and his enforcer Pappy Mason; his top lieutenants, including his sister Viola, were beginning their descent into drug addiction. Worse, Viola was going in and out of jail with the frequency of a low-level hustler, because she was bagging and transporting drugs herself. A big no-no when she was supposed to be running things for Cat.

Cat was facing numerous charges, including weapons and drug charges and the murder of his parole officer, Brian Rooney. Pappy was in jail for the Rooney murder also. The state had airtight cases against them, if only their witnesses stood fast. But with Cat's and Pappy's aura of menace, prosecutors weren't confident their cases would hold up. Perry Bellamy was one of the star witnesses, but he was scared to death.

Bellamy was in no hurry to testify against either Fat Cat or Pappy. "There's not a single soul who is gonna come in and testify against that boy. The Fat Cat has become more powerful in prison than he ever was out on the streets. He's got the name Perry Bellamy on a contract too, no doubt about it." A local said. In fear for his life, Bellamy lived on Rikers Island in protective custody.

Bellamy's father, Alonzo, a 50-year-old father of six, who worked at Wilken's Quick Wash and Dry on Linden Boulevard, wanted no part of his son or the drug business. He was just a civilian, but that didn't stop Cat's gun thugs. Alonzo was doing his job as usual, pushing a broom through the laundromat when a young man entered the rear of the store. There were no words, just the gunshot- one slug hitting Alonzo right between the eyes. The old man lingered for a couple of weeks at Mary Immaculate Hospital, but he never regained consciousness.

"I was asked to kill the witness that was going to testify on Fat Cat about his parole officer murder," Glaze said. "The dude that was going to testify was in jail in P.C. so we could not get to him, so I had to kill his father. I murdered him in a laundromat and asked him for change so I could use the machines. When he gave me the change I put my gun to his head and murdered him. So his son took back his story and Fat Cat beat the charges."

The hit on Mr. Bellamy was only part of the plan, detectives learned. The rest of the plan called for a grieving Perry Bellamy to be gunned down at his father's funeral. The kid was smart enough to stay in jail. Since they couldn't get to him in protective custody they tried to maneuver him into a position where he could be touched. Pappy and the Cat meant business.

Violence in Queens, especially in witness intimidation cases, was quickly becoming a Bebos trademark. In another incident, Pappy's young soldier Shocker allegedly bashed a woman to death with a cast iron pan. "I told you about running your mouth," Shocker told the woman as he allegedly beat her head to a pulp. With loyal soldiers still on the street, the imprisoned drug lords were trying to reclaim their dominance. Fat Cat and Pappy Mason were not playing when it came to their freedom or their money.

Prosecutors and judges weren't immune to threats either. The judge in Cat's guns-and-drugs trial, from the 1985 raid on his storefront, had his life threatened repeatedly leading up to, and during the trial. He had been under police guard for months. Fat Cat was doing everything he could to get out from under the indictment.

The prosecutor, Warren Silverman, was also living under a death threat. In Pappy Mason's case the prosecutor and judge were living under constant anonymous death threats during the weeks prior to the trial. Right before the trial began, the star witness Perry Bellamy refused to testify. Pappy had gotten his man. He was laying the precedent for his defense also.

"Me and Pappy was in Queens House together and he told me, 'I didn't kill no parole officer.'" Luc Spoon said. Pap denied that he arranged the murder. "Hell, no." He said. While Pappy was getting witnesses to clam up or eliminating them, Cat's case progressed to trial. After numerous delays it was time to face the music.

"Nichols is one of the major drug dealers in all of New York City," Queens District Attorney John Santucci said. "His operation netted millions of dollars annually and extended beyond Queens into Brooklyn and Nassau County." Cat's prospects didn't look good at the guns-and-drugs trial.

A jury deliberated for more than two days after the 10 week trial in Kew Gardens, Queens presided over by State Supreme

Court Justice Vincent Nero, before finding Nichols guilty on three counts of criminal possession of a controlled substance and six counts of criminal possession of a weapon. The Cat was sentenced to 25-to-life on the charges. *Nichols is convicted on Drug Charges, The New York Times* headline read on January 9, 1988.

The Cat held his face in his hands as the sentence was read. Fat Cat, having been indicted for killing Rooney in July 1987, still faced a murder trial and a second life sentence. One of the cops attending the trial yelled, "The Cat's nine lives are over. Nobody takes an order from a lifer." In this great moment of triumph for law enforcement, none of the cops could imagine the sorrow that would come.

"When we were locked up together, Cat went on trial for his drug case." Prince from the Supreme Team said. "He started acting a little shaky. His fear of blowing trial and going back up north was tremendous. He had numerous enemies waiting on him. In January 1988, Cat blew trial; I was in the dayroom watching TV when he came back from court. He went straight to his cell. I found it strange that he went straight to his cell.

"As I'm passing by his cell, I stopped and asked him was he alright. He looked up at me and I saw tears in one eye and tears rolling out the other. I told Cat, 'Don't worry about that shit man. Preme took a nine-to-life and gave it back on appeal, you stand a better chance cause you went to trial.' Afterwards I warned Pap, if you don't distance yourself from Cat he's gonna use you as his ticket out of prison to avoid going up north."

Pappy followed the Cat to trial, but without Bellamy willing to testify, only his taped confession was played for the jury. The jury was deadlocked at nine to three for a conviction, when the judge declared a mistrial. "Pap went to trial and had a hung jury. He had a hung jury on the murder." Luc Spoon said.

It was an eventful week in South Jamaica. The cops had won a big victory over Fat Cat, but Pappy beat them in a stalement. "Pappy didn't kill no P.O. He actually got two mistrials," D says. "Actually the three people who killed the P.O. are in the feds now." Following his mistrial in the Rooney murder, Pap remained in jail on the gun charge. But he would make bail and when he did, all hell would break loose in Queens.

CHAPTER 6

Cop Shot

New York streets where killers walk/like Pistol Pete and Pappy Mason/Give the young boys admiration. Nas, Get Down, Gods Son (2002)

Pappy Mason made bail in February 1988 after the hung jury. Without a live witness willing to testify the jury wouldn't convict him. The prosecutors were scrambling, trying to find a way to keep him incarcerated, but they were at a loss. The wheels of justice turned, and Pappy hit the streets.

He knew he wouldn't be on the street long, the feds and the state were building numerous cases against him, so he was busy trying to get his and Fat Cat's business in order. In the process of doing so the world turned upside down. A fateful encounter on the street would change everything on the Southside of Jamaica, Queens.

It would end up effecting criminal justice policy, the federal drug laws and law enforcement's agenda. A confrontation between Pappy Mason and a beat cop named Bobby Kisch would spark the flame that engulfed Queens and ignited the War on Drugs, mandatory minimum sentences and politicians' tough on crime rhetoric. Pappy Mason's antics would end up causing a ripple effect that would affect hundreds of thousands.

Kisch, a burly white cop who lived in a Queens housing project, was considered one of the 103rd Precinct's most active cops. At age twenty-five, he was a throwback to a different era. Kisch, nicknamed "The Iceman", had a reputation for street toughness. He took it personally when dealers congregated on his beat and used force to move them along. Just after Pappy made bail, Kisch came upon him in the street. Pappy was standing on 150th Street and 109th Avenue in South Jamaica drinking a can of beer. The police officer approached him, demanding respect.

"Do me a favor," Kisch told Pappy. "Don't drink beer in front of me. Put the can in a paper bag." Pappy Mason was stunned. No cop had ever spoken to him like that. All the deep rooted hatred Pappy had for authority figures rose to the surface. He was furious. He was surrounded by his fellow Bebo members. All Pappy's cohorts were watching to see how he would react. Pappy talked the talk, but now everyone wanted to see if he walked the walk. Pappy was nothing on the street without respect. "Do you know who I am?" Mason asked.

"Yeah," Kisch said. "You're the guy who's gonna put his beer in a paper bag." Mason's comrades began to walk off. This was in the parlance of the street, a situation. They didn't want to be around when it jumped off. Pappy Mason was liable to do anything.

"Fuck you," Pappy told the cop, bringing the beer to his lips. Kisch pounced, pushing Pappy against a metal window guard. "You either put that beer in a bag or I'm gonna arrest you for disorderly conduct. Who do you think you are talking to a cop like this?"

Mason threw the beer in a garbage can and walked off the block. His cohorts taunted the cop, insisting Kisch had made a grave mistake. Mason said nothing until he was off the block. Then he turned to a friend and said, "That cop has to die. He dissed me." And Pappy Mason wasn't prone to making idle threats.

Within a week, Kisch was called in off the streets. A

supervisor had explained to Kisch that it was just too hot to have him out there. The Bebos had put the word out, "Get the Iceman," and they made sure the police knew about it. "We're getting too many death threats against you," Kisch was told. "The word is that Pappy is going to kill you."

Fearing a bloodbath and considering Pappy was putting hits on policemen, the Queens District Attorney's Office quickly got Mason off the streets. They didn't dare leave him out there to enforce Fat Cat's will or to follow through on his death threats to the cops. He was remanded after only 10 days in the free world and rushed to trial on a weapon possession charge.

But it was too late; Pappy had already formulated a plan that would set in course motions that would shock the nation. "Pap got bail in January 88, but only for a week and they revoked it because they said he was trying to blow up the 111th Precinct," D says. "He wanted to leave his mark on the precinct. The young cop got Pap in his feelings. Pap was telling everyone that would listen that the cop would pay." Law enforcement didn't realize the extremes that Pappy was willing to resort to.

"When Pap went to jail, most of Cat's strength in the streets was gone." Prince said. With Pappy back in jail for good it seemed dudes on the street started feeling themselves by attempting to make their mark in the drug game. Cat's rivals recognized and attacked where it would hurt Cat the most.

While Pappy was making plans to strike at authority, instead of handling the crew's business, rival gangsters were moving in on Cat and Pappy's territories, and letting it be known what they thought of the Cat. With the prolonged absence, the fear had abated and Fat Cat's empire crumbled. It was a war of attrition and Cat was losing.

The Cat's string of bad luck continued when his sister Mary perished in a firebomb attack on his mother's home, and though the crime was never solved, rampant speculation abounded. Everyone from rogue police officers exacting revenge, to rival dealers from Brooklyn targeting Cat, emerged. But it could have been anyone.

A car full of gun thugs screeched to a halt in front of Cat's mother's house at 114-21 139th Street at 12:30 a.m. Louise Nichols, 71-years-old, was sitting on a couch in the living room. She turned to see a firebomb crash through the window of her three story frame house.

A gun thug in a multi-colored jacket sprayed the burning wood home and family cars with automatic gunfire from about 150 feet. He fired at least 16 shots from an automatic weapon. Some shots struck two cars belonging to family members and others hit the front of the house.

In the house were Cat's stepfather, Amos Coleman, 70-years-old, and two of Cat's nieces and a nephew. After the attack the assailants sped off. Fat Cat's mother survived the attack, but the drug lord's wheelchair bound 50-year-old sister, Mary Nichols, died in the fire.

Mrs. Coleman told reporters that she had tried to help her daughter, who had suffered a stroke, out of the house, but Mary was too heavy in her wheelchair and she couldn't be removed in time. She died in the house. Cat's nephew suffered burns on his arms, but everyone else escaped injury.

The police said that they didn't know who was responsible for the attack, but they thought the incident was related to the drug wars in South Jamaica. A police spokesman said the area had been "relatively quiet" since Fat Cat and Pappy Mason's incarceration. But things were starting to heat up. Law enforcement figured with the two notorious gangsters locked up things would calm down. They couldn't have been more wrong.

Fat Cat was upstate, at Shawangunk prison, serving a 25-to-life charge, while awaiting trial that he ordered the murder of his parole officer. Pappy was at the Queens House of Detention for Men awaiting trial on the gun charge. With the drug lords on ice, their grip on the area loosened. With no shot callers to rein in the wolves, chaos ensued.

Cat desperately wanted to go to the funeral, but he was not allowed. He sent a weepy message from jail, which was read at the service. "If in any way I'm the cause of this, I'm sorry, because you know I would most definitely trade places with her," Fat Cat wrote. "I never took the opportunity to tell baby sister I loved her. Now it's too late." The letter, which was read by Reverend Charles Norris during a sparsely attended thirty five minute service in a St. Alban's funeral home began, "Dear Momma."

Fat Cat was furious with police, who said it was too dangerous for him to attend the funeral. "This is just another way of them trying to torture me by not letting me say goodbye to my sister," Cat wrote. "Times like these is when a family really needs to stick together. As I'm sitting here, writing this, I keep thinking about baby sister. If there is a heaven, she's there."

As Norris read the letter, he stood a few feet from a three foot tall floral exhibit of red roses in the shape of an "S"- a tribute from Supreme and the Supreme Team to Cat. The Cat still had his support in certain areas, but many were turning on him. All the setbacks were wearing on Cat.

At a hearing, he looked a little fragile. He didn't stay long enough to hear the judge rule that there was sufficient evidence to go ahead with the charges against him for the Rooney murder. Obviously, he didn't care. He'd already asked to be taken back to his cell, saying he wasn't feeling well.

To Cat the writing was on the wall. He was feeling the full effect of his actions and dreaded the inevitable consequences. With his confidence and swagger gone, his crew was staggering like a punch-drunk champ, about to take his first knockout loss. The streets were watching to see if the Cat could make a last minute stand, but the odds were against him.

Neighborhood people said Nichols' crew was no longer an important force. The power they once held was waning. On the streets the signs that Cat's reign had ended were visible. Big Mac's, which used to be his headquarters, was still open, but drunks, who would have been chased away before, hung around the outside, and people who went in came out carrying actual groceries. "He isn't Fat Cat anymore," a local said. "Long live the king, the king is dead."

The attack on his family, coupled with the kidnapping of his wife a year earlier had destroyed him in the street. At age twenty nine, he was a vanquished emperor. Police theorized that the bombing had been done for the conviction of Richard Frejomil on charges of kidnapping Cat's wife, Joanne.

A police department spokeswoman said the possibility that Frejomil's conviction was related to the firebombing was "as good a theory as any." She said the conviction of Frejomil, who was awaiting sentencing, was "the most recent, visible thing to come up" in the South Jamaican drug wars. With Pappy off the streets, all of Cat's enemies were coming out of the wood work and looking for revenge.

Other detectives believed the bombing had been ordered by Brian "Glaze" Gibbs. Glaze, cops said was attempting to take over the Fat Cat/Pappy Mason network. Police said that a man described as black, 6-foot-tall and 175 pounds, wearing a multicolored jacket and hat, had been seen down the block, close to the spot where shell casings were later found. Glaze was believed to be the gunman.

But Glaze refutes this; he was working for Fat Cat at the time and wanted to murder those responsible for the firebombing. "I wanted to kill their mothers, their girls and their kids, but Fat Cat told me that would be too much killing," Glaze said. "I killed one of the guys at a Chinese restaurant in Carnegie. He firebombed Cat's mother's house. When those dudes threw the firebomb in Cat's mom's house and it killed his sister did they have remorse or was the guys that kidnapped Fat Cat's wife off the streets remorseful. I don't thinks so. I set an example out of anyone that went against us."

It was unclear to police who threw the firebomb and no one was ever charged. Police said the man left the scene in a four door Buick Electra. Police found five weapons, including a .9 mm and a .22 caliber semi-automatic rifle in the house, along with a file cabinet and two safes. None of the residents of the house were charged in connection with the weapons. Everybody knew the guns belonged to Fat Cat.

While Cat was reeling, Pappy was plotting revenge. But he was plotting revenge on the wrong people. Pappy had a serious problem with authority. In his mind he thought if he took on the biggest gang in New York, the NYPD, he would prove his superiority over the streets. Pappy wanted to send a message that he was the baddest gangster around. Wishful thinking on his part. Enter Arjune.

When the man known only as Arjune and his family moved into a vacant three-story house at 107-05 Inwood Street and 107th Avenue, South Jamaica in September 1987, the double lot was overgrown with weeds and littered with whisky bottles and vials of crack. Arjune, a Hindu from Guyana, cut back the brush, cleaned the lot and had the house painted and remodeled. He put a small American flag in a lighting figure next to the door.

Inwood Street, which ran south from Liberty Avenue, was a narrow street, with two story houses that were fairly well kept on 45 by 100 foot lots. The area was a working class section divided equally between whites and black families until crack hit the scene, and drove away all those who could afford to move out.

"These are nice people here," a local woman said. "Most of these people work. Most have families. It was a nice neighborhood until they started with these drugs on the corner. Now this is a bad neighborhood. A lot of crack. A lot of bad stuff around the neighborhood."

The arrival of crack and Fat Cat's demise opened up the market for small-time hustlers. The result was a level of competition unheard of among Queens more traditional drug traffickers. Before prospective dealers had to be invited to participate in the drug game. Crack enabled anyone to get into the game.

As the feared Pappy Mason and Fat Cat were put away, other hustlers stepped in to fill the vacuum, testing their mettle against each other to see who was the baddest. "They're not battling the police," a cop said. "They're battling each other." Their battles were measured by the higher levels of murders and shootouts, which consumed and engulfed the area. Terrifying the residents, not only in the poor areas of the borough, but also in the affluent neighborhoods near the Nassau County border. It was a free for all.

"There's no monolithic structure here," a local cop said. "There's a lot of independent organizations who are vying for the best locations and customers." With Fat Cat's conviction, instead of celebrating the police began mobilizing to fight the crack plague in Queens.

Between October 1987 and January of 1988 there were 2350 arrests for the sale and possession of drugs, along with the seizure of 10,744 vials of crack and thousands of dollars in cash and quantities of heroin, cocaine and crack. The police conceded however, that their efforts had barely scratched the surface of the problem. They also discovered a bloody paradox in their enforcement efforts.

"We've come down rather hard on them and took out their leadership rather rapidly," the cop said. "And while that sounds great and we've gotten some convictions and some of them will be sent upstate, that also has left the organizations in disarray, causing them to scramble to put new leadership in place. And so the war will go on. Drug dealers are like hydras. You cut off the head and another grows back."

Arjune, in the middle of the crack war chaos, decided to fight back. He wasn't dissuaded by the atmosphere of intimidation created by the drug crews. He was sick of his block being overrun with crackheads and dealers. Every time he went out his front door it looked like an open air drug bazaar.

In fact, his home had once been a crack house where cops performed buy and bust operations. The area had a storied history in the drug trade, being only half a dozen blocks from Fat Cat's former headquarters at 106-60 150th Street. Arjune had no idea he was living in crackhead control.

Arjune made it a point of pride to call the 103rd Precinct to complain about dealers, users and lookouts. He even fancied himself to be an informant of sorts. Local dealers, mostly remnants of Fat Cat's old crew, led by one of his lieutenants, Thomas "Mustafa" Godbolt, had taken over the area.

Mustafa had a stronghold in the neighborhood called the Blue Fortress with a thick steel door, surrounded by a cinder block wall on 154th Street and 107th Avenue. His crew was angered when Arjune's complaints led to the arrest of 20-year-old Yusif Abdul Qadir, a neighborhood resident, busted for possessing six vials of crack. Mustafa decided it was time to strike back.

Hours after the arrest of Yusif, two low level enforcers working for Mustafa, and by proxy Fat Cat, tossed three Molotov cocktails at Arjune's home. As police were arresting 27-year-old Claude Johnson for the attack, three more Molotov cocktails were thrown through Arjune's window.

But before the fiery, homemade bombs could do any serious damage to him, his family or his property, Arjune, who was awake waiting for the attack, picked up the incendiary devices and threw them back out the window. Robert Webster, a 17-year-old neighborhood kid was arrested for the second attack. Both assailants were charged with menacing Arjune, among other charges.

The police, up in arms, and feeling the sting from recent criticism for not protecting witnesses, took an unusually strong action and placed an around the clock police presence outside Arjune's house. The message to perpetrators was that another incident of this kind wouldn't be tolerated.

The 24 hour guard outside Arjune's house did little to impede the crews operating nearby, who simply went about their business while steering clear of Arjune's home. It was business as usual for them. A sense of security returned to the street, but it would prove false.

Meanwhile Pappy was busy implementing his plan to send a message of his own. "He was out before they remanded him. He was organizing at that time." A local said. Pappy was angry because after he beat the P.O. murder rap, he was sent back on the gun charge, for a tiny derringer pistol. Hardly something a real gangster should be held accountable for.

Pappy was ready to take it to trial, but there was a strong possibility he would lose. Not something he was accustomed to. This increased his anger, making him furious. The fact that he was in jail for a little pistol was crazy to him. He was the big, bad Pappy Mason, he shouldn't be held on a gun charge.

On Tuesday February 23, 1988, a Queens jury convicted Pappy on the gun charge. Upon hearing the verdict, Pappy turned to the prosecutor, Scott Tulman, and formed an imaginary gun with his hand and index finger. Then Pappy pulled the trigger. Law enforcement didn't know it, but this would be the symbolic shot heard round the world.

After the attack on Arjune, Fat Cat's crew should have refrained from committing more high profile acts of violence, but Pappy and his loyal crew of Bebos viewed the firebombing of Arjune's house as the opening salvo in a wider war on law enforcement and those who cooperated with them. It was do or die with them.

Pappy's greatest flaw was his irrational hatred of cops. He'd go on tirades about cops that stretched so long that listeners had little idea of what he was talking about. Pappy's rage even baffled the Bebos, a group hardly inclined to like the police, as they were subjected to daily pat downs, searches and arrests. They just took it as Pappy being Pappy.

"It was already planned," Scott Cobb said referring to the hit. Pappy put the hit on Bobby Kisch, the cop who had dissed him. "Not saying it would be that cop, but a cop. Whatever cop that was going to be in that area. That's how they had it, that's how it was. Pappy was the man who delivered and gave the order to Marshal, Philip Copeland. Pappy's the chain of command. Then Marshal. He told him, 'I want this person knocked, whatever, boom.'

"They got a thing that they call 'One love', and when Pappy say you do, you do. One love mean 'we do or die.' This is how they think. One love, one love mean, 'Hey, we all fight. We all family. I give you an order, you do.' On the phone, when Pappy calls, his name is Bebo. We don't call him Pap on the phone cause the phones be tapped. Just say, 'Bebo.' That's what we call him on the phones. They'll all talk Jamaican. They slur and you couldn't understand what they were saying. But I would understand what they was saying on the phone." Scott Cobb said.

But Shocker contradicts Scott Cobb, "One love don't mean do or die, one love means peace and love. Just like when people say love is love. Scott Cobb wasn't a Bebo; he just got caught up in the mix."

From Rikers Island, Pappy called his trusted Bebo lieutenant, Marshal. "We lose one, they lose one," Pappy said, signing off with the Bebos "one love." To a Bebos insider like Marshal this cryptic call was crystal clear- take out a cop. It's said Marshal went to see Pappy and received a gold and diamond ring shaped like Africa, worth 40 grand, off his finger in the visiting room at Rikers Island. Cops surmised this was payment for the hit.

"Pappy felt when he went back to jail, they had to pay for that," Cobb said. "There was a thing behind Fat Cat too. They said that 'We lose one, they lose one.' This is what they were saying and they said that there would be more. This is what Marshal been saying. They saying, 'Cat got twenty five to life, boom!' He had nothing to lose. So Pappy knows he's facing time, it's, 'Let's send out a message.' That's the message. That even though they behind bars, they still give orders and it be done."

During a follow up call, Pappy made $8000 available for the Bebos to do the hit. Marshal was good with the ring but the other Bebos in on the hit would have to split the $8000. They didn't care though, they were happy to have an opportunity to serve Pappy. He was like their lord and they were his soldiers.

Marshal decided the perfect mark for the job would be whatever cop was guarding Arjune's house. Not only was the police presence an affront to the dealers and Cat's crew in the area, but the lone policeman would be a sitting target. It wasn't the cop Pappy wanted, The Iceman, but it would have to suffice.

"Marshal knew a cop always sits there alone," Scott Cobb said. The police officer would spend his shift reading a newspaper or watching a portable television set. Marshal found this to be an opportunity he couldn't resist. He knew the game changing aspect of the murder would elevate the Bebos to the boss crew on the Southside of Jamaica, Queens. Rival dealers and parole officers had been slain, but a cop guarding a witness had never been done and would up the ante considerably.

On February 25, 1988, Marshal gathered fellow Bebos Todd "Divine" Scott, Scott Cobb and David McClary at an apartment in the Forty Projects. The crew plotted the execution and decided to draw straws to see who would be the triggerman. No one volunteered for the volatile mission.

"It was supposed to be seven people open up on the whole car. We surround the car, open up on the car. We had the car timed when Pappy was out here. They said the car was marked. David scouted the area. He was the one who planned it." Scott Cobb said. Todd Scott drew first and came up with the shortest straw. "It looks like it's you." Marshal said to Todd. "We ain't got time to waste."

With a murder mission on their mind, the Bebos had to arm themselves. They stopped by Cobb's girlfriend's home at 108-44 160th Street to pick up a .357 Magnum. They got a two door 1979 Dodge with tinted windows from a heroin addict and stopped by a Jamaican gun dealer to buy bullets. They had a drink at a nearby bar on Liberty Avenue and Remington Street to bolster their courage and then drove up Inwood Street by the police cruiser.

"He's sleeping, he's sleeping." Cobb who was driving said. "That's the one," added McClary. Cobb parked the Dodge about a block away from Arjune's house, at Pine Grove Street and 107th Avenue. Todd then allegedly led Marshal and McClary toward the police cruiser as Cobb remained in the still running Dodge.

As traumatic and personal as the loss of his sister was, it was the murder of a total stranger that would completely up end Fat Cat's world. Working the overnight shift on February 26, 1988 a 22-year-old rookie police officer named Edward Byrne sat in his squad car performing a routine guard duty on Arjune's house.

Byrne, was approached by someone who knocked on his

window at around 3:30 a.m. When he turned to look, someone approached the driver's side. What happened next would shut down New York. Byrne looked right and caught five in the head. Byrne, a second generation police officer, lay dead in his cruiser. "It was literally an assassination," Curtis Scoon said. "Everybody was shocked."

As the news spread through the ghetto, incredulity descended on the street in the neighborhood of mostly black and mostly working class and poor residents. Accompanying the slaying were feelings of unfairness and intimidation and the sense that no one was safe, not the citizen who complained about drugs, nor the armed officer assigned for protection.

"I heard three shots," a local said. "I didn't think nothing of it. I didn't think anything like this could happen. Who's going to be shooting with a cop on the corner?" The brazen slaying of the rookie officer was seen as an outgrowth of the crack epidemic which engulfed South Jamaica, Queens and became a symbol of all that was wrong in the borough and in the nation.

More than $20,000 was offered for the capture of the shooters. At 8 a.m. on the morning of February 26, 1988 Queens Narcotics Detective Mike McGuiness got a call from the station. "We're all working on that cop killing. Last night they shot a cop." An officer told McGuiness. "You're kidding?" McGuiness couldn't believe it. But his mind was racing.

"It's gotta be Fat Cat," he told the officer. "For two reasons, first the week before, Fat Cat had just been found guilty on state narcotics and weapons charges and second, Pappy was arrested on gun charges. Plus Arjune's house was just a block away from Cat's grocery store."

The officer on the line seemed skeptical. "Informants are telling us that the killing was done by a group of Jamaicans from Brooklyn who wanted to take over the territory." In the first days after the killing, theories were plentiful as to why and who.

Police Commissioner Benjamin Ward called the slaying, "a deliberate assassination," apparently aimed at sending a message to anyone willing to fight back against crack. With the scene of the shooting on the southern fringe of the area around Sutphin Boulevard, 150th Street and South Road, the coordinates marked roughly the drug headquarters of Fat Cat. With the close proximity, obviously he took the blame, as police sought to place guilt for the shooting.

"We're living in times where your life don't mean nothing," a local said. "And it's terrible in a place like the United States to live that way." Law enforcement officials looked closely at the possibility that those behind the killing of Officer Byrne were the same people believed to have been behind the earlier efforts to intimidate the witness he was guarding.

Thomas "Mustafa" Godbolt, who was convicted of criminal weapons possession in 1982 and was awaiting trial on charges of giving the order to have Arjune threatened, was a suspect. Mustafa, who had a nearby home on 157th Street near 107th Avenue, was a Fat Cat lieutenant and was holding down the area for the incarcerated drug boss, police said.

"He's either an associate of Fat Cat or is operating in that area with Fat Cat's permission," a cop said. To law enforcement, everything still ran through Fat Cat. The police officer's death stunned and rocked the local residents, who were fed up with local drug dealers and their antics. They expressed their outrage.

"Here's a young boy," a woman from the neighborhood said. "He had a nice face, a sweet boy, sitting there doing his job, protecting us. He didn't do anything to them. Why did they have to bother him? I said hello to him several times. Nobody wants to feel uncomfortable in a neighborhood, no matter what color you are. Somebody has to get to the root of this. It's not fair. How could people do such evil things for no reason?"

In the minds of the Bebos they had a sure fire reason. Even if it wasn't rational. They were striking back for the home team. It was an "us against them" mentality that Pappy had foisted upon them. And the enemy to their way of life was the police. It was cut and dried to them; still the murder sparked a media frenzy. *Battle for Crack Trade in Queens May Hold Key to Officer's Killing* and *Living with Violence: Disbelief and Fear Shake South*

Jamaica were two headlines *The New York Times* ran in the aftermath. The surprising thing was, before the police officer was killed, the papers barely mentioned Fat Cat or Pappy Mason. But after the murder their names dominated headlines for the next several years.

The officer was just four days past his 22nd birthday and other cops called him rookie. His career was just beginning, and it was already over, as was his life. It was a tragic incident that spurred the police to action. More than a thousand cops hit the streets of South Jamaica in search of Byrne's assassins. They would not rest until the guilty factions were found.

The killing prompted an inquiry in which 250 police investigators working 12 hour shifts blanketed three precincts-the 103rd, 105th and 113th in southeastern Queens. They conducted more than 200 interviews at almost as many locations and questioned more than 300 suspected drug dealers.

A telephone tip hotline was set up to receive information from the public and produced 350 calls in the first day. The calls and informants reported all types of scenarios on the killing. There were no secrets in the streets. The streets were talking. People always want to label others as snitches, rats or informants, but the reality of it is that people tell on other people. That is just how it is. People like to talk and whether it's direct or indirect, it's people that are telling.

Teams of police officers swept through crack houses in the area searching for leads, while detectives sifted through hundreds of telephone tips on the special hotline number. At least 14 people were arrested in Queens, but there was no indication that any were directly linked to the slaying.

One Hundred Fiftieth Street, the block, was shut down and thousands lined the streets of Queens for the funeral procession. With the block shutdown and the spots closed, the crackheads were fiending. The pressure being applied by police was relentless and it wouldn't take long to find the assassins.

"The Bebos done it. They shoot all their enemies in the head," an informant said. Still another informant said, "Tommy

Mickens did it. He's mad because the FBI is after him now. They got this big case going against him." Another informant stated that he had heard someone named Kandu discussing the hit. "Kandu was saying that he had to stay low and get his stuff off the street because Prince and his boys were talking about hitting a cop. The word in Forty Projects is that Prince and his boys did the hit." The snitching was not left to men alone. A C.I. named Missy was in Queens Women's House of Detention when Fat Cat's niece Pumpkin told her, "They took one of ours, so we took one of theirs. Abbie did it. Blew the guys head right off his shoulders." Another informant said, "A female named Jackie told me that Fat Cat could only call on three people to do the job. One is named Bugout, the other is named Mike Bones and the third is named Todd." Still another man arrested on a drug charge said, "This is the kind of thing the Bebos would do." Speculation was rampant.

"They fucked up." A local said. "The unwritten cardinal rule is don't kill a cop. The reason being, it disrupts all operations. Touch a cop and the whole force will be out for revenge." With Cat locked up and Pap on his way upstate the position of power was vacated. There was a vacuum to be filled.

There were those who had watched Pap rise and they wanted a taste of the respect and power Pap and Cat held. There were many applicants to the throne. The position of drug lord was highly coveted. To gain it prospects to the crown would create mayhem. Blood was running along the sidewalks of Queens and dudes were fighting for position. *Weathering the Crack Storm in Queens* was the headline *The New York Times* ran to describe the scene. The gun thugs were out for blood and if the cops got in the way, they were fair game also.

Early on police missed opportunities in the investigation. In the first hours after the killing detectives had grabbed James McCaskill, Todd Scott's friend who was called Homes. "Homes stated that he knows Mustafa from the neighborhood, and his brother Saleem," a detective wrote. "He further states that he does not know anything regarding the police officer that was killed and did not hear any word on the street."

At the time of his capture, he was arrested for having a couple vials of crack, Homes had just walked out of Carmichael Diner, leaving Marshal, Todd, Scott and David sitting in the back booth. It was a narrow miss for the police. But there were others.

A cop from the 75th Precinct who was investigating a different murder had just picked up a suspect in east New York. The suspect was Fat Cat lieutenant and Viola Nichols' cohort Glaze. Glaze was in his Jeep at a grocery store on Lincoln Avenue, between Sutter and Blake with two others, who just happened to be Marshal and David McClary. Their names meant nothing to the cops in the 75th Precinct at the time.

All three were taken down to the station. Glaze was booked on the murder charge and cops interviewed him and the others concerning that homicide. McClary took a seat in the interview room. All around him cops were talking about the Bryne murder. "If I see these guys I'd just shoot them down. No questions asked." One cop said.

Their comments unnerved McClary, but Marshal had very little to say. He sat down on a detective's desk for a while and laid down, sleeping in the middle of the squad room. Due to the cop killing, the east New York cops called in Queens detectives to talk to Glaze. He refused to talk with them. "The police questioned me whenever any murder happened in east New York, but nothing ever stuck." Glaze said. As an afterthought the detectives interviewed Marshal and McClary.

McClary, a former basketball star in the Police Athletic leagues knew getting down with the Bebos was good business. Knowing Todd and Marshal was a good look. They were the power brokers in Queens. McClary wanted money for gold and clothes, he wanted to be somebody people would notice. He had finally achieved his goals, but the cops made him nervous.

In an effort to cover his tracks he told the detectives, "I know the drug dealers because I live in the area. I like Fat Cat cause he gives me money to buy sneakers to play ball. I know Pappy sells drugs on 150th Street and Sutphin. Skinner sells drugs, but he's a nice guy. I don't like Mustafa. If anyone killed the officer, it should be Mustafa."

Marshal didn't say much, he told cops he knew Fat Cat, Pappy and Ruff, he said he ran errands for Pappy's mother while Pappy was in jail. He said on the night of the murder he was with Audette Wills at Kennedy Inn Hotel on North Conduit in room 504. The two men, having posed for photographs, were getting ready to leave when the 113th Precinct called to say they had a warrant on Marshal. He wouldn't be leaving. But Marshal knew the paperwork game. He was looking at an overnight stay in jail, nothing more.

As David McClary left he asked Detective John Califano, who had questioned him on the cop killing for a ride back to Queens, but the detective told him, "I don't think that would be possible." With all the information pouring in the cops missed what was right in front of their face. Until one of their main informants, Billy Martin, spelled it out for them.

The cops had photographs of all the suspects on a wall in the homicide office. Fat Cat, Skinner, the Corleys, Mustafa's people. Pappy's picture was up there, Marshal's picture and Todd Scott's. Billy walked in the homicide office.

"What are you fucking around for?" Billy asked. "You know this man here had to call the shot," pointing to Pappy. "And you know he called Marshal and Marshal took care of it. You know Marshal took Todd with him, because that's his main man." The cops asked Billy, "How do you know that? Who told you?" Billy said, "I didn't hear it from nobody, but that's the way it works and that's the way it's gotta be."

The cops called the lieutenant in. They had all the manpower at their disposal. Over 100 detectives were in that squad room, the informant ran over it all again. The lieutenant made the decision that one team would focus on Mustafa and Bugout and the task force would focus on Todd and Marshal.

It was apparent from looking at it on the surface that Mustafa had the cop done because of Arjune. He had the most to lose, but a lot of the force had wanted to prove that Fat Cat ordered his crew to deliver a dead cop. So they focused on all fronts until they got better intelligence and more specific information. Getting that intel didn't take long.

An anonymous man called from a phone booth saying that he knew "who shot the cop, because his friend works for the drug dealers who were responsible for the murder." The caller was nervous. The detective who took the call convinced the anonymous tipster to meet him at the corner of 95th Street and 57th Avenue in Maspeth. The detective and a uniformed officer met the caller and drove him to the station; he started talking in the back of the patrol car.

"I'm involved with the drug dealers that killed the police officer," Martin Howell said. "Todd Scott killed the police officer on the orders of Pappy Mason." Howell was taken to the homicide office, where the photos hung on the wall. He walked immediately over to a picture of Todd Scott.

"He killed the cop," Howell said. "He is the shooter." Howell then pointed to a picture of Philip Copeland. "We call him Marshal. He was involved too. There's another guy named Scott. You don't have his picture up there, but he was involved too. They drive a 1979 beige Chrysler two door with tinted windows." Martin Howell then went on to detail the facts as he knew them.

"The night before the shooting, in the clubhouse with me were Marshal, Todd, Scott's uncle, Darry and Stevie O. Todd announced that the boss Pappy, wanted a cop hit, that there was $8000 a head for the job. I thought they were kidding. They started sniffing coke and drinking beer. They drew straws. Marshal and the two Scotts drew straws. Todd picked the short one, so he had to do it. After that I went home.

"Friday morning I woke up. Turned on the TV and saw the news about the shooting. I went outside and saw Scott all flashy, new clothes, big gold chains, showing big knots of money. When we got to the clubhouse, there was Roger and Kevin. Scott started saying how it happened. How Todd came up to the car asking for directions and pulled out a sawed off shotgun and shot the cop five times. Marshal then came to the club and said the same thing. Then he said, 'Business as usual,' and not to say anything about it." The cops were putting it all together and building a case file.

In their reports detectives wrote of the informant: "Subject belongs to the Bebos. They hang out at a location in the Forty Projects. There is one member whose first name is Scott. Scott's uncle is legal tenant of the apartment in the project where they hang out. Thursday before the shooting Todd Scott, Scott Cobb, Philip Copeland, Stevie O, Darry (Copeland's cousin) and Kevin Curry were present in the room when Todd Scott makes an offer of $8000 to kill a cop.

"The order to hit a police officer was given by a big dealer who is presently in jail and goes by the name of Pappy. It is common knowledge among the group that there is a police car with a police officer guarding Arjune's house around the clock. On February 26, the morning after the shooting subject asks Cobb, 'You all did it?' And Cobb answers, 'Yes.' Cobb says that when Todd blew off the cops head he was laughing. Subject said that Cobb had told him the cops brains were splattered all over the front seat of the car."

With this eyewitness account the cops started building their case. Their informant Billy came back with some new information also. He had been in a car with Marshal and Todd. Billy said Todd knew they were looking for him. He was held up in an apartment on Guy R. Brewer Boulevard and South Road. Todd was very bored. He told Billy, "You gotta get me some Nintendo tapes. I need something to do during the day. They're looking for me and I don't have anything to do up in the apartment." Billy got him the tapes.

Finally the suspects in the cop killing were arrested. Within days, four suspects that belonged to the Bebos were arrested and charged with the murder. Todd Scott and Scott Cobb were picked up after investigators, working closely with cops of the 103rd Precinct, developed information leading them to Todd Scott, 19-years-old and Scott Cobb, 24-years-old.

Detectives converged on a two story frame house at 93-

08 209th Street in Queens Village to apprehend the first two suspects. Scott Cobb emerged from a side door and Todd Scott was hiding with two women in the basement closet. Two more suspects were arrested the next day. They were identified as David McClary, 22-years-old and Philip Copeland, 22-years-old.

David McClary surrendered to the police in the Queens Village station house in the 105th Precinct in the company of his mother. He was the only one of the four not to have a record. Philip Copeland was already on Rikers Island for failing to answer a bench summons. They rearrested him there and took him to an interview room to read him his rights.

"I suppose you guys are going to beat the shit out of me too," Marshal told the detectives. "No, you know we don't work that way." The detective said. They then started asking Marshal about Pappy Mason. "I ain't got nothing to say about Pappy." Marshal said. The detective told him, "I understand that Cat's losing all his juice on the street. Pappy's got the upper hand."

Marshal smiled at that and started talking about the Round Table ring. He was dressed in a tan leather suit. He had this big ring on his finger with a map of Africa on it. The ring was adorned with a big diamond. The detective asked Marshal where he got it and Marshal told him Pappy, but that was all the cops got out of him. When they pressed him further he told them, "I ain't no Perry Bellamy."

All four suspects were arraigned in Queens on charges of second degree murder and criminal possession of a weapon. All four were held without bond. "We're pretty satisfied the key players are taken care of," the Police Commissioner said. "And the important thing now is to continue the investigation and make sure the person or people who originated this idea are arrested and prosecuted."

Police Commissioner Benjamin Ward said that the men were hired to kill Officer Byrne in order to send a message that no one who interfered with the drug trade was safe. Police described the suspects as "street punks." One local woman said, "I'm surprised they killed a cop. But as for drugs, that's just the neighborhood."

The cop's murder shocked the nation.

"I'm sitting in Clinton. I see the news about the police getting assassinated. I think right away, I hope it wasn't these niggas." Luc Spoon said. "It was our neighborhood. Ain't nothing going on in that hood unless it's someone we know, its somebody that you know because it's your neighborhood."

Three of the four suspects made videotaped statements implicating each other; another claimed Cat ordered the hit from jail. As law enforcement pressed them, they spilled their guts on the murder, implicating anyone they thought the cops were interested in. "Now you tell me," Cat said. "On one hand, they say I'm so smart and on the other they say I did something stupid. Which one is it?"

One of the men, it's still not clear to this day who, as they all implicated each other in the shooting, pumped several bullets into Byrne's head, killing him instantly. Cobb, who named McClary as the triggerman, said that right after the killing Todd peered inside the window of Byrne's cruiser and burst out laughing.

"Todd said the first shot hit the officer and he seen his brain come out," Cobb said. "Then Todd said one of the bullets almost hit him because it came through the door. Then David told Todd to come on because he was still laughing." The only Bebo of the four to keep his mouth shut was Marshal, who claimed to be at a girlfriend's house the night of the murder.

"The cops lie on him because they know he help all the youth of Queens who were Bebo get out of prison. Marshal is a Ras I love," Pappy said. The other three Bebos couldn't resist talking. They bragged and boasted of the assassination. They were high on murder.

"We rocked that nigga," Todd boasted. "I am the baddest motherfucker around. Nobody can stop me now." Scott Cobb strutted through Forty Projects, where he proclaimed, "You gonna hear about me, fuck that." At the time no one knew what he was talking about.

"Todd Scott and them niggas are from the projects. Forty Projects." BC Says. "Everybody wants to be a ghetto superstar, that's what we figured. We didn't know 'bout the cop until the next morning. But when you got a motherfucker with an ego as big as a building ain't no telling what he may do."

The morning after the cop was hit Marshal picked them all up and took them to breakfast at Carmichael's Diner on New York Avenue, behind Baisley Projects. They decided to lay low at Pappy's safe house in Queens Village, but first they divided up the $8000 for the hit and went shopping, bragging about the hit to a store clerk. The clerk was excited to meet the high profile Bebos.

"You guys from Queens are really bad," he said. "Killing cops." Todd humbly accepted the compliment. "The cop was younger than me. He had his gun right across his lap. I could see his blue eyes." He replied.

As the police were looking for leads, the streets were talking and their talking led police right to the perpetrators. At the same time, the feds were conducting an investigation on the Fat Cat organization, and what they heard on their wiretaps confirmed law enforcements theories.

Agents had listened in as dealers in Cat's crew complained about the police pressure on their business following the cop killing. In one such conversation Viola Nichols wondered whether Pappy Mason had gone over the edge. "He's my man and everything," Viola said. "But why he do that stupid shit."

The dude she was talking to, Glaze said, "He mad." Viola agreed, "Yeah. He mad. Do you think he did it for the weight to fall back home or do you think he was a Goddamn fool?"

Viola raised a valid point, because while Pappy was deeply loyal to Cat, Byrne's murder was perceived by Fat Cat as a powerful act of sabotage that literally killed Cat's organization. Could there be some Machiavellian power play going on?

"The purpose of the cop's killing was to bury Cat," D says. "Pappy wanted to make sure Cat didn't come home. He tasted power, real power while Cat was away and he never wanted to give it up. By getting the cop killed, he knew the weight would fall on Cat." But if so it was a big miscalculation because everyone would take the weight.

"That was the beginning of the end. I wasn't home for that I was locked up." Shocker says. "Perhaps that was a good thing, because I might have been a suspect for that. Even to this day they saying that Todd Scott, David McClary, Philip Copeland and Scott Cobb did it. They got convicted for it, but nobody knows if they really did it. If I was out I would have got 25-to-life too."

Law enforcement was taking down every one that was Fat Cat or Pappy Mason related. With the killing of one of their own, the real war was on. It was game time for law enforcement. They wanted to find out who called the shot. The papers agreed with this assessment as they ran the headline, *Mastermind Sought in Officer's Killing.*

Edward Byrne became a symbol of unity for law enforcement in New York. "The murder of Edward Byrne was a culmination of the terror the dealers put on the neighborhood and put a spotlight on the Southeast Queens drug trade. The hammer comes down on the whole South Jamaica drug scene. The police were like 'we're not gonna take it anymore.'" Ethan Brown said. "Every time there was a flashpoint in the drug crisis, whether it was Fat Cat in 1988 or Len Bias' death in 1986, you have lawmakers scrambling to put more people in prison for longer periods of time."

Pappy Mason had impacted American culture in more ways than he could have ever imagined. He made history and changed the course of current events. The actions of Fat Cat and Pappy Mason single handily brought on the War on Drugs and mandatory minimum drug sentences. Their actions ushered in the prison age in the United States and led to millions being locked up for drug crimes.

Nearly 10,000 cops, including the entire 103rd Precinct, attended Byrne's funeral at St. James' Church in Seaford, Long Island on February 29, 1988. It was the largest turnout for a fallen colleague in the history of the NYPD. Eight cops carried Byrne's coffin, which was draped in the green and white flag of the NYPD into St. James as *When the Battle is Over* played. The coffin was followed by Byrne's father, Matthew, a former police lieutenant and close friend of U.S. Attorney Rudy Giuliani.

Mayor Koch gave a speech immediately following the funeral in which he said Byrne's death was as of an important a milestone as the passing of Martin Luther King Junior and John F. Kennedy. "If drug traffickers have become so emboldened that they can engage in the assassination of a young police officer, then the whole of society is at risk and we will have anarchy," Koch said. "That is why his death rivals the others. Not because he is Edward Byrne, but because of what it means to have this police officer assassinated."

As cops continued to hunt down crack dealers in their purge the Southside of Jamaica Queens struggled to come to grips with the fact that the city's streets had almost succumbed to lawlessness. *Police Broaden Queens Drug Crackdown, The New York Times* headline read. As the police took back the streets they celebrated their victories where they found them.

The city's Irish cops, a number that had once included Edward Byrne had great cause for celebration on St. Patrick's Day 1988. Even as the Emerald Society bagpipers were making their first appearance since the Byrne funeral, marching down Fifth Avenue a roar was being heard a borough away in the Kew Gardens Courthouse on Queens Boulevard.

Pappy Mason, wearing dreadlocks and a white sweater that looked to be an Irish knit, stood beside his attorney C. Vernon Mason. The attorney, no relation to Pappy, had earned a reputation as a champion of black rights. He had just represented a black teenage girl who claimed to be raped by white police in a New York town named Wappinger's Falls. Even though the claims were proved false, the racially explosive story made the lawyer's name.

In his defense of Pappy Mason, the lawyer said his client had been framed by police and called the conviction racist. Making it a racism thing clouded the real issues. Good tactics for the defense, but the judge was not impressed. Pappy was resigned to his fate.

"You gotta do what you gotta do," Pappy told the judge. "I look crazy, so people are going to judge me on that." Although Mason had not yet been convicted in the Rooney slaying or even named publicly as a suspect in the Bryne assassination, he felt compelled to discuss the killings at his sentencing for the gun charge.

"This is two cops I supposedly, allegedly killed," Pappy said. "Cops come to me at the precinct and say I'm the leader of a drug ring. I've never been arrested for drugs in my life. I don't know what they're talking about."

The judge sentenced Pappy to three-and-a-half to seven years on the gun conviction. But really it was just a pretext, more severe charges were being prepared. As Pappy was led away, the prisoner turned to the prosecutor, Scott Tulman. "Jive ass," muttered the ever defiant Pappy Mason. As Pappy was returned to prison, the community he destroyed was coming to grips.

"We want it to be like it was when everyone was decent and respected each other," a local said. "We want peace. These are good and decent people here and they've tried so hard, but they're scared. These young punk dealers have no regard for life whatsoever."

Living in the midst of such violence had made neighborhood residents prisoners in their own homes. "Sometimes you have to fight your way out the door," a local woman said. "Because they're standing there, leaning on your gate." On summer nights, gunfire was heard regularly and local residents felt like they were living in the Wild, Wild West.

Despite the vigorous police presence, the boulevard remained an ominous place where drug dealers stored their Uzi's and AK-47 assault rifles in apartments above the bodegas. The local playground at the nearby Public School 48 had become the weekend province of drug dealers holding court and selling their wares to all comers. The area was awash in the crack plague.

Young children were faced with the dangers of the streets and teenagers were recruited to work for the drug lords so they could buy bomber jackets, Air Jordan's and removable gold grills for their teeth. All local symbols of sudden, ill gotten prosperity. Crack culture had taken over, despite the police presence. The temptations to do wrong and court chaos were all around, and the youngsters easily succumbed to them. The lure of the dope game saturated the neighborhood and residents were sick of it. "We've got 16-year-olds here making more money than their fathers and mothers combined." A local said. "It's ridiculous."

Bryne's murder brought more than a heavy police presence to the streets of Queens. It spurred a national conversation about the failing War on Drugs and the rising crime rates in America's major cities. Mayor Koch ran a full page ad in *The New York Times* headlined, *Officer Edward Bryne was Murdered in Cold-Blood. Let's Make Certain He Didn't Die for Nothing.*

"We are truly in a war with the drug pushers," Koch said. Other media outlets perpetrated the hype. *Newsweek* ran features on the theme titled *Losing the War?* The attention from media and politicians enabled the NYPD to take a much more aggressive stance in the Southside of Jamaica Queens. Koch announced the formation of the Tactical Narcotics Team, the 118 member TNT unit set up their headquarters in Arjune's house.

Arjune was becoming a hero to the public himself. The immigrant's bravery had become part of the national dialogue. "If the police stay here and they keep the dealers out of the neighborhood, this will be a beautiful place to live," Arjune said. "I don't want to go back to Guyana. I want to stay in America. If something belongs to you, you should stand up and fight for it." For almost two months, the 1.6 square mile section of South Jamaica became an occupied territory.

With Arjune's house at the center, the neighborhood became a laboratory for an experiment in law enforcement for the TNT unit, whose purpose was to disrupt the increasingly brazen and violent drug trade in the streets. TNT was announced at a City Hall news conference on March 7, 1988 in the aftershock of the cop killing. The audacious crime, officials decided, required an ambitious response using their full force of all city, state and federal agencies to rid the area of drugs, especially crack.

The city had declared war on crack dealers and the Southside of Jamaica Queens was the battle ground. Achieving that lofty goal seemed near impossible. But in interviews police officials, residents, civic leaders and elected officials, who represented the area, agreed that flagrant drug dealing had been decreased dramatically and that the police operation had reassured a measure of order to the neighborhood which had grown fearful.

"The police were like the infantry," a councilman said. "They cleared the field, but cleaning up the drugs is just the first step. To hold the positions, you really have to have the federal programs come in to eliminate supply and demand." Police officials buoyed by a police survey of 59 residents who praised the effort, expanded the territory of their operation.

The new zone, which included the original boundaries of South Road and Sutphin, Baisley and Merrick Boulevards, covered 5.5 miles, three times the original area. Through the first couple of weeks of the crackdown, 630 arrests were made. Of the 630 narcotic arrests, 429 of them were made by TNT officers. Of those 429 arrests, 337 were felony arrests, the overwhelming number of which involved crack.

A far reaching benefit of the arrests of the low-level drug dealers was the information that the TNT unit gathered on the streets. The snitches were running their mouths to gain their freedom. The arrest of high echelon distributors by the Joint Narcotics-FBI Taskforce was imminent. It seemed progress was being made.

"I don't know if you could consider the drug trade down to a trickle yet, but it's not the river it was," Captain Ryan Thomas, commanding officer of the TNT unit said. "There is an improvement. We are getting fewer complaints about narcotics activity, about a quarter of the calls we were getting before TNT. When I go through the district, I see less visible loitering and congregating on the corners, which are indications drugs are being dealt."

Locals reported feeling a whole lot safer. "There was an arrogance about these drug dealers," a woman said. "It was, 'To hell with the decent people. We're going to take care of business.' That flagrant attitude is gone." The locals, sick of being under the drug lord's power, were seizing the streets back.

"The neighborhood was fantastic until the drug trade started to wreak havoc on the streets, closing small businesses and causing those remaining to cage themselves in." A local pastor said. The feelings he expressed were held by a lot of residents. Especially with the brutal murder. There were always a handful of community people who helped the police, but the cop killing produced a new brand of involvement.

"This is the first time I've ever seen actual bonding between community residents and the Police Department." A cop from the 103rd Precinct said. "Usually, even with good people, it's us against them and we're perceived as the occupying army. But this incident here made them see us as victims too. They know this precinct suffered a loss and they're reaching out to us."

Dozens of letters of sympathy arrived at the shabby station house where Officer Byrne's name would be the fifth on a brass plaque honoring officers who had been "called to rest." One neighborhood woman sent a poem expressing her sadness that, "just as we got to know him he made the greatest sacrifice." The poem was mimeographed and was placed throughout the building and was sent to the Byrne family.

On the streets in the immediate vicinity of the killing, residents spoke of their grief and their hope that Officer Byrne's death would have redeeming value. The ferocious response by local, state and federal law enforcement officials and the sudden attention of politicians vowing a serious crusade against drugs was a change for the better, residents thought.

"What has struck many of us is the current determination to make an absolute fight of it." A local said. "All of a sudden lots of important people are saying, 'This is it. This is where the train stops.' We hope through his passing that other people will come to live in peace and safety. Perhaps the purpose of his life will be to salvage this neighborhood."

Edward Byrne's father was emerging as a tough vocal opponent to Queens drug crews. His political emergence and personal crusade galvanized law enforcement and politicians alike. On the day after Arjune spoke of American values, Matt Byrne and his family visited the Inwood Post. Arjune and Byrne met on the spot where his son was killed and bowed their heads in prayer.

"I think people are finally coming to realize we are losing the drug war," Matt Byrne said. "Eddie's murderers need to be pitied and prayed for. They do not know the sanctity of life. They cannot really know or understand what they have done, even though it is such a terrible sin."

The police commissioner, Benjamin Ward, dropped a bomb shell during a speech also. Arjune was going to be given a new identity and enrolled in the federal witness protection program. The city had agreed to pay him $126,000 for his house and troubles. Arjune became one of 5,153 federally protected witnesses. Only three percent of those people were law abiding citizens. "It is the right thing to do," Arjune said. "I can't live here anymore. I am stepping into a world of darkness."

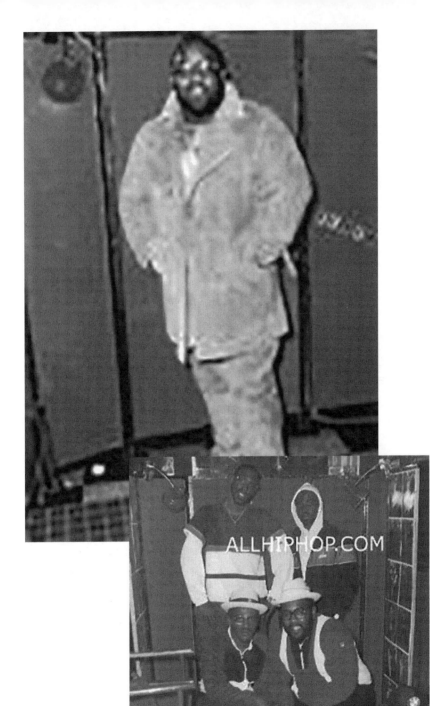

CHAPTER 7
Fed Case

Fat Cat's Empire Crumbles: Feds Bust Drug clan,
$20M Dope Seized, 30 Suspects Nabbed in Massive
Raid. The New York Daily News

As the witch-hunt gathered momentum; other law enforcement agencies such as the FBI, U.S Attorney's Office and the NYPD were investigating, building and bringing cases against anyone remotely associated with the cop killing. It was a bonanza for law enforcement, as they were given free rein to do as they pleased, in regards to the Queens drug dealers.

The cop killing was a call to arms for law enforcement as a whole and they answered the bell, ready to knockout the Queens drug dealers, no holds barred, UFC style. Law enforcement wasn't holding anything back. As the cop killing investigation kicked into high gear, Queens prosecutors fired their first volley.

Attacks on Witness Detailed at Trial, The New York Times headline read on August 13, 1988. A Queens prosecutor described a night of terror for a South Jamaican homeowner to the jury. The prosecutor, James Liander, told of the fire bombings in his opening statement, at the trial of two defendants charged with hurling gasoline bombs at the house.

The two defendants, Claude Johnson and Robert Webster, were charged in the trial at State Supreme Court, with arson and other crimes. Mr. Liander told the jury that they "threw Molotov cocktails, incendiary devices, glass bottles filled with gasoline and a wick, at a wood frame house owned by a Guyanese immigrant" the aforementioned people's hero, Arjune.

"Two Molotov cocktails made it into the house," the prosecutor said. "Arjune picked them up and threw them back out." The prosecutor said that Arjune, who emerged from events as a symbol of citizen determination to resist drug dealers, was burned slightly, and his home was lightly damaged by the attacks. Both defendants, who were jailed without bail pending the outcome of the trial, lived near the Arjune house at 107-05 Inwood Street. Arjune was scheduled to emerge out of the federal witness protection program to testify at the trial, and at two other trials of people accused of threatening him. The defendant in one case was Mr. Webster's father, who was charged with witness intimidation. The other defendant was Thomas "Mustafa" Godbolt, who was charged with coercion and menacing. Authorities linked Mustafa and the other hoodlums to Fat Cat, and even though the Byrne killing was not mentioned in court, it cast a dark cloud over the events.

The feds investigation of Fat Cat was ongoing and the cop killing only added fuel to the fire. Even though four suspects were arrested on state charges for the killing and would be tried in state court, the feds had something up their sleeves for the two they considered the primaries, Fat Cat and Pappy Mason. The feds were preparing the knockout blow, but on Uncle Sam's team it wasn't all kosher.

There was a lot of dissension in the ranks of law enforcement as the feds got their case together. Some state authorities and NYPD members felt the feds were dragging their feet. Most of the Queens detectives felt cheated by the federal case. They also suspected that the indictments could have been announced in January, 1988. A full month before Byrne's murder. With the

Cat in jail for 25-to-life and Pappy in jail fighting cases, the federal case was anti-climatic. The feds even stole the NYPD's informant, Billy Martin.

"The FBI was all over the place, looking to hook up with the guy," the Queens detective said. "We used to see him every day. We used to meet him in different places. We wanted to do a whole in depth investigation. Set up a task force, get wiretaps, everything. We wanted to, but the state couldn't use him, because he flunked a polygraph. The District Attorney John Santucci made the decision himself. This decision had the net effect of getting Edward Byrne killed. No doubt about it.

"I wouldn't quit on Billy. I sat him down. I told him, 'Look, we can't use you, because we can't give you any money. We're nickel and diming you to death. With the information you've got, you gotta do it right. Do you want to go with the feds?' Billy said, 'I'll go with the feds.' So I called the narcotics guy, Sergeant Mike McGuiness and said, 'Make us an appointment. We'll take him down there. You sign him up.' He signed an agreement with the feds and asked for a Chevy Blazer. He'd be put in a witness protection program when it was all over.

"The feds used Billy to start building an entire RICO case. He did everything for them. He got them into everybody. This agent named Ray Byers was running the investigation. He loved Billy as a C.I. Billy did all the introductions for the FBI. They got Billy on film with Cornbread and Hymie. Billy was able to bring in undercovers and introduce them to all the guys."

Scott Cobb agreed to cooperate with the U.S. Attorney also, which led to a massive federal indictment against Cat and Pappy. The feds were building their case, but since they were flipping dudes left and right, they kept adding counts to the indictment by handing down superseding indictments. The feds were stacking up the charges on Cat's crew. They were applying the pressure and wouldn't let up. A byproduct of the cop being murdered.

Law enforcement, both federal and state, were out for retribution. They had their sites clearly targeted on Cat and

Pappy, and anyone associated with them. The heat was coming down like a flaming inferno and there was no place to hide or get away. Everyone associated would end up getting scorched. The only way to avoid the burn was to flip and cooperate. Divide and conquer was the feds' tactic and they worked it to perfection.

Nearly six months after the Byrne killing the police got the Nichols family together. A team of FBI agents and Queens Narcotics cops moved in to smash the drug ring. The campaign, code named Operation Horse Collar, was a culmination of information supplied to the government by the NYPD's informant Billy Martin.

Thirty Held in Sweep Against Drug Ring Tied to Officer's Killing, The New York Times headline read on August 12, 1988. After making an enormous undercover purchase of 70 grand worth of heroin near Big Mac's Deli from Fat Cat's distributor, Man Sing Eng, in late July 1988, the feds moved on Cat's crew. The crew was reduced due to all the cases, but Cat kept the business going by drafting all of his relatives into the operation.

The fact that his whole set up was being run by his female relatives, was a testimony to the stature and respect Cat still held, on the street and in the hood. His influence was monstrous. Even though he had chinks in his armor, he was still able to operate his empire, up until the day of the federal indictments.

More than 400 police officers and federal agents began arresting suspects at 6 a.m. in a sweep of 21 sites, many of them in the sections of Jamaica, Queens that the Nichols group used as bases. Five parcels of real estate were seized, in addition to money, drugs, shotguns and machine guns. Anything of value the feds could get their hands on was seized.

Properties at 150-02 107th Avenue, 115-32 155th Street and 105-06 150th Street, as well as several apartments above it, were seized and identified by the feds, as either headquarters of the Nichols operation, drug packaging sites or retail spots. *U.S. Marshal's Seize Drug Locations in Queens and Brooklyn, The New York Times* headline read.

Federal agents also served search warrants in upstate New

York, Maryland, Virginia and Alabama. The feds said by the time the investigation was completed they expected to confiscate more than 30 parcels of property, mostly real estate investments, bought with profits from drug sales.

Cat wasn't playing. He was taking a lot of money off the block, from his retail drug sales operation, and he invested this money in real estate. The feds found out about a lot of the land and houses, but not all of it. It's said Cat still has land and property, bought during his run, to this day.

"The Byrne murder was a catalyst to those of us in law enforcement," U.S. Attorney Andrew Maloney said. "Whatever made them commit that insane act of murder, surely backfired on this organization. This has led to the demise of the Nichols organization."

To many inside the law enforcement community, the calculated murder of a police officer broke one of the unspoken, but cardinal rules generally respected by the drug underworld in this country- don't kill the police. Without a dramatic response, some officials feared attacks on law enforcement would escalate, as they had in Colombia and other Latin American nations.

The federal complaint charged Fat Cat, Pappy Mason and 35 other people including Joseph "Bobo" Rogers aka Mike Bones, Karolyn Tyson, Louise Coleman, Amos Coleman, Char "Shocker" Davis, Chris "Jughead" Williams, Luc "Spoon" Stephens, Man Sing Eng, Marica Nichols Williams, Paris Williams, Ida Nichols, Carol Craft and Martha Craft with operating a $20 million dollar drug organization that was responsible for at least 10 murders. Among those charged with conspiracy to distribute drugs were Cat's mother, father, sister, three nieces and his girlfriend.

"It's appropriate that families that commit crimes together should serve time together," Police Commissioner Benjamin Ward said at the news conference held at the 103rd Precinct in Jamaica, announcing the arrests. The police said the arrests were intended to demolish the organization headed by Fat Cat, a man they described as the dominant power in heroin and cocaine distribution in Queens.

According to the complaint released by the U.S. Attorney in Brooklyn, Fat Cat, who had been in prison since November 1985, continued to direct drug operations through telephone calls and visits from lieutenants and family members. For years, the authorities said, members of the Nichols' organization terrorized the poor and middle-class black neighborhoods in Queens with public murder and wanton violence.

Although no murder charges were filed, a criminal complaint made public, cited unidentified informers as saying the Nichols' organization was responsible for the Byrne killing. The complaint also said the Nichols' organization was responsible for the 1985 murder of Brian Rooney, Cat's probation officer.

Fat Cat himself was rearrested the day of the raid and moved by federal agents from his cell in Wallkill State prison in upstate New York, to administrative segregation at MCC New York, the federal lockup in Manhattan. His whole crew was there, more than 30 enforcers, runners, lieutenants and suppliers, with names such as Jughead, Ninja, Bugout, Shocker and Mike Bones.

The arrests included the mothers of Fat Cat and Pappy Mason, as well as their girlfriends and sisters. An assistant U.S. Attorney, Charles Rose, handled the indictments. He taunted Pappy Mason and Fat Cat in an underground parking lot as they were being led upstairs to be arraigned on the federal charges.

"Look," Rose said to Fat Cat and Pappy. "There's some other people upstairs that you know." Pappy asked, "Who?" Assistant U.S. Attorney Rose said, "Your mother." And turning to Fat Cat, "Yours too." Rose's move had the desired effect. Pappy Mason quickly made a threat to the prosecutor.

"Pappy Mason wants to have me killed for arresting his mother," Rose bragged to agents. In the world of federal drug enforcement, a prosecutor wasn't anything until his life was threatened. Pappy Mason's threat put Rose on the map in the world of federal law enforcement. It was a feather in his cap.

The Fat Cat organization was what the DEA considered a mid-level drug organization. It was nowhere near as large or sophisticated as the industry's top level organizations: Mafia and Chinese groups that imported heroin into the city, or the Colombian cartels that controlled most of the world's cocaine supply. But the brazen violence by members of Cat's crew, as they vied for territory in Queens, brought them national notoriety. Authorities said Fat Cat hired executive officers, comptrollers and security people who sold $10 and $20 dollar bags of heroin and cocaine from a half dozen outlets in Queens, Brooklyn and Nassau County. The conspiracy charges stemmed from an investigation started by the DEA in 1986.

Cat's crew and the Bebos had a reputation for the quick executions of competitors, at times burning them with gasoline. It was believed they were involved in the spraying of gunfire on two crowded street corners in July 1987. The violence perpetrated by the crew was legendary both in scope and brutality.

Even though Fat Cat tried to distance himself from direct sales, he was a common sight at neighborhood drug locations prior to his incarceration, offering youths a frightening, but alluring symbol of the rewards of life in the drug trade. Bedecked with gold, gorgeous women by his side and riding around in luxury automobiles, the Cat was a walking promo for the dope game. Impressionable neighborhood residents clamored to be associated with him.

One of those arrested with Fat Cat was his sister, Viola Nichols. Viola was very brave at the time of her arrest, kicking and spitting at a television news reporter, who stuck a microphone in her face. She was the epitome of the angry young woman, but that would change shortly.

Her boyfriend, Fat Cat enforcer Glaze, was arrested also. Glaze's operation had been doing decent business on the streets of Brooklyn, but couldn't compare in sheer size and profitability to Cat's crew. He was just one facet of many sub-organizations under the Cat's influence. To the feds it didn't matter, they were moving in on everyone associated with Fat Cat and Pappy Mason. It was a full court press, a ground and pound of epic proportions.

"When he got busted in 1988, he had been in prison three years. They seized $20 million in drugs and 30 people were arrested, and he was running that from behind bars." Curtis Scoon said. Some said prison enhanced Cat's criminal stature. His power was evident, but the feds didn't care, they had plans to break him.

The feds were trying to leverage the arrest of Cat's 77-year-old mother to make him copout, but Cat was weighing all his options. He didn't want to go out like a punk and then there was the street code to consider, but he knew the odds were against him. The Cat was trying to exercise every one of his nine lives to find a way out of his predicament.

His options weren't looking good, as everyone connected to him and Pappy was locked up and put in prison. "It was Pap, it was Cat. They all went down. Pap's momma went down; Cat's momma went down, everybody." A local said. Darryl Littlejohn aka Johnny Blaze was a worker on Cat's team. He started to snitch on players from the hood team, working as a C.I. Johnny Blaze wasn't the only one to flip. When the pressure came, a lot of people couldn't stand it.

Within hours of her capture, Viola cut a deal with the feds. With the cop killing trial not yet begun, the NYPD were very interested in what she knew about the murder. "When the feds made the arrest, we went back to 26 Federal Plaza and they bring Viola in. The feds wouldn't let us talk to her." The Queens detective said.

"This guy, who is an assistant U.S. Attorney comes in and says, 'I'll go in there and talk to her. And if she says anything worthwhile, I'll come out and let you guys know.' So we were on their turf, but we've had it up to here with their government bullshit and FBI secrets. So the U.S. Attorney comes out about half an hour later and says, 'She's not really saying anything. She's just talking about this guy Pappy in jail.'

"You could see the cops and feds squaring off up there. One detective on the Byrne case asked, 'Do you know who Pappy is?' It was obvious the attorney didn't. He was just grandstanding. We had been waiting months to hear this. There was a lot of tension up there that day.

"They had a lot of our guys working on the federal case. I thought there was going to be a fight. No New York City cop respects a fed. The FBI doesn't trust us or share info with us. But they can't get the job done without us. And it turns out Viola has got plenty to say." Viola Nichols made a full statement to the feds and NYPD on August 15, 1988. The following represents that statement.

"Understanding all my rights, I make the following statement concerning what I know about the murder of Police Officer Edward Byrne. I returned home on January 11, 1988, after being in jail for approximately two years. At that time Howard Mason, who I have known for approximately six years, was in jail in the Brooklyn House of Detention.

"I know Howard Mason by his street names, which are Bebo, Pappy or Star. Pappy was released from jail approximately one week before Police Officer Edward Byrne was killed in Jamaica Queens. Pappy returned to jail on Thursday, February 15, 1988, the day before the officer was killed. I know it was a Thursday, because it was the day after my regularly scheduled visit to my parole office.

"During the week that Pappy was out of jail, he came to my house everyday so that he could receive phone calls from my brother, Lorenzo Nichols, whose street name is Busy or Fat Cat, who was in jail. Usually with Pappy were two men I knew as Philip, also known as Marshal and Todd. On one or two occasions Pappy came with Scott. On several occasions Pappy met David McClary at my house.

"I have known Philip for approximately three years. I have known David McClary for many years. I was introduced to Todd and Scott by Pappy during the week that he was out of jail. After Pappy went to jail and until the four of them were arrested, I continued to see the four men everyday. They usually drove a green Jeep.

"On August 11, 1988, I was shown photographs by Detective James Waddell of the New York City Police Department. I identified those photographs as the four men I know as Philip, also known as Marshal, who I now know to be Philip Copeland; David McClary; Todd, who I now know to be Todd Scott; and Scott, who I now know to be Scott Cobb. I signed and dated those photographs on August 15, 1988. Everyday until they were arrested, the four men came to my house, usually between 6:00 and 6:30 p.m., so they could receive telephone calls from Pappy.

"The night Pappy was returned to jail, February 15, 1988, Philip Copeland and Todd Scott came to my house to wait for such a telephone call. Pappy called at the scheduled time and spoke with Philip Copeland. Most of the conversations was what I call, Bebo talk, and I couldn't understand it. However I did overhear Philip asking whether he should contact Bobo, who I know to be Mike Bones. I learned that Bobo was not to be contacted.

"Police officer Edward Byrne was killed on Friday, February 26, 1988. Within the next two days I received telephone calls from my mother Louise Coleman and my sister-in-law Joanne Nichols, in which they told me that Busy, my brother Lorenzo Nichols was mad about what, 'That stupid motherfucking Pappy did.' At first I didn't understand what they were talking about. When I asked, my mother and Joanne told me that it was about, 'That stupid shit Pappy had done.' My mother told me that it was about the killing of the police officer and that Busy was very mad at Pappy.

"A day or two after I spoke to my mother and Joanne; I got a call from Busy. During the call Busy asked me whether I had spoken to Bebo yet. I told Busy that I hadn't and Busy then said to me, 'Man, I don't know why Bebo did that fucked up shit. What Bebo did was fucked up. He messed up everything for everybody. Now nobody will make no money. Now he won't make no money either.' I understood from the conversation that Busy was talking about the killing of Police Officer Byrne.

"One or two days after I spoke to Busy about the police officer, Pappy called me. I asked Pappy, referring to the murder of Officer Byrne, 'Why did you do that?' Pappy told me, 'You don't understand. The man dissed me.' I told Pappy over and over, 'I still don't understand why you did it.' Pappy kept telling me that it was because the police officer dissed him by ordering Pappy to put a can of beer that Pappy was holding in a brown paper bag. "Within the next day or two I again spoke with Busy. At the time Busy told me that, 'Pappy had the wrong fucking cop killed.' On what I believe to be the second Sunday after the murder, and after the arrest of the four men, Pappy called me from the Brooklyn House of Detention, Pappy told me to tell Homes, who I know to be David McClary's friend James, 'to get the thing clean, the prints off and break it up and get rid of it.' I understood 'the thing' to mean the gun used to murder Officer Byrne. Because I didn't want to be involved, I told Pappy that he should tell Homes himself. Pappy told me to find James and that he would call back.

"I beeped Shawnee, who is David McClary's girlfriend and told her to tell James that Pappy wanted to speak with him. A little while later, James came up to my house and the two of us waited on Pappy's call. I answered and gave the phone to James. Then Pappy had a conversation, which I didn't overhear. After the conversation I asked James what he was going to do. James told me he was going to do 'what Bebo told me to do.' James then left.

"A few days later, after the telephone call between James and Pappy I saw James on the block. I asked James, 'Did you get rid of it?' Referring to the gun and James told me, 'Yes.' Prior to the telephone call between Pappy and James I asked Shawnee, 'Did David do that?' Referring to the murder of Officer Byrne. Shawnee told me that David had done it.

"Shawnee also told me that the police had come to her basement window and she had fled. She told me the gun was at her house and after the police had left she hid it somewhere in the neighborhood. There are additional details which I could provide concerning my conversations with people named in this statement, this statement is only a summary of those conversations. Signed, Viola Nichols."

Viola's statement would make the case for Queens detectives. It also put Pappy Mason front and center for a new federal indictment. With everything going from bad to worse for Fat Cat, it seemed his whole world was turning upside down. Queens biggest drug dealer had taken a big hit, but more startling ramifications were still to come. First though, Edward Byrne's murderers would have their day in court.

Byrne's Slaying Called 'Symbolic Message', The New York Times headline read on February 22, 1989. The day after what would have been Edward Byrne's 23rd birthday, the trial of his killers commenced. His parents, Matthew and Ann, stared somberly ahead in the spectator section as assistant District Attorney Eugene Kelly made opening statements in the case. He called the suspects "agents of death" who were delivering a "symbolic message."

That message was that the crack dealers were "above the law and that if you interfere with them or interfere with their leaders, they will shoot you" even if "you happen to be dressed in blue." Mr. Kelly was dramatic, even theatric as he presented the case to the jury.

"There were five shots that were heard on the streets of Jamaica," Mr. Kelly said in State Supreme Court in Kew Gardens, "and ladies and gentlemen of the jury, they were five shots that were felt across America."

The lawyer for Scott Cobb said in his opening argument that his client was not guilty, because, although he had driven two of the accused killers to the scene, he had done so "without knowing what would happen. There's a difference between being at a location and being involved in an incident that caused the death of another." The lawyer, Michael Fishman said.

As his husky, bespectacled client watched without expression, Mr. Fishman attacked the credibility of prosecution witnesses, many of whom, he said, had criminal records, for charges such as larceny and drug dealing, and had made deals with the authorities. All four defendants were charged with second degree murder, the highest murder charge possible under state law, which was punishable by a maximum sentence of 25-to-life in prison.

Another prosecutor Kirke Bartley told jurors that the four accused men had carried out the killing at the direction of Pappy Mason. But Pappy had not been charged with involvement in the killing and he denied the accusation. "Why would I kill a cop?" Pappy questioned. Prosecutors said Pappy, who was thrown in jail two days before Officer Byrne's slaying, was "a boss who was not going to let going to jail go unanswered."

The prosecution presented its first piece of major evidence- a videotape statement in which Todd Scott gave detectives and a prosecutor a graphic, chilling account of Officer's Byrne's death. In the statement, made shortly after his arrest, Todd Scott admitted to having been at the scene, but insisted that David McClary had done the shooting and told police he had gone along because he didn't believe McClary was serious about murdering a police officer.

"I went to the scene to see what happened," Todd Scott told police. "I just seen the first bullet hit him. I saw his head down and his hair flying like, you know, like a blow dryer. I seen the blood and stuff." The videotaped confession was detrimental to the defendants.

Scott Cobb, in his statement to authorities, put himself at the scene and said McClary had been the gunman. McClary, in his statement, admitted he was there, but said Todd Scott had fired the .357 Magnum hand gun. Marshal was the only Bebo of the four not to make incriminating statements to authorities. He held true to the street code and stayed loyal to his boss Pappy.

Marshal was a soldier to the end, while the other three Bebos crumbled under the police onslaught. They couldn't withstand the police pressure. When they found themselves alone in the interrogation room, they broke weak. But others broke weak and testified at the trial also, including Darry Newby and Martin Howell, fellow Bebos.

"Todd Scott was talking to Philip Copeland and Scott Cobb," Newby said. "He said, 'We have to kill a police officer.' The other two nodded their heads in agreement." Howell testified that

"Marshal asked Scott Cobb did he have the jammies," explaining that jammies was "street terminology for gun." He said Scott Cobb responded that he was going to get the "artillery" from another member of their crack trafficking gang.

In his testimony, Howell suggested that Pappy Mason had given the order to kill an officer, he quoted Todd Scott as saying that "the boss put out an order to hit a cop, and whichever one of us was to participate will receive eight grand." Howell did not say who "the boss" was, but earlier testified that he was a drug dealer "with the Bebos." *The New York Times* ran the headline, *Witness Recalls Talk of Desire to Kill Officer.* The media was hyping up the story.

Scott Cobb, in his statement to police said Pappy Mason was the "bossman" of the drug gang and was called Bebo by his underlings. Numerous other witnesses and law enforcement officials were called to the stand to testify. But it didn't matter for the perpetrators, because their own words had hung them. If they would have kept their mouths shut they might have had a chance, but Marshal was the only one who didn't talk.

About the trial Marshal said, "They say that me and Pappy planned this, but me and him never talked and I didn't go see him, so I can say that he didn't play no part in it. All three of my codefendants made confessions only implicating themselves, also stating that I played no part in this crime. And they also explained each others roles in terms of who did what. As far as bosses were concerned, there was no boss with us, every man was for himself.

"I look at it like this, they used me and my boy to make points during the election year. I was in the hotel all night with my old girlfriend Audette Wills, which she confirmed on my behalf during trial. All witnesses were paid sums of money by the district attorney's office to testify against me. Martin Howell, Darry Newby testified to taking money and the prostitute Rachel Moore was the only one to put me at the scene of the crime. She constantly changed her stories and was still paid."

Prosecutor Kelly, in his closing statements apologized

for the world he had showed the jurors- a world of deceit, ignorance, violence and evil, the world of Martin Howell, Darius Newby and Rachel Moore- the crack world of South Jamaica, Queens. It was only through these witnesses' eyes, and their voices, Kelly argued, that the world of Todd Scott, Scott Cobb, David McClary and Philip Copeland could be revealed.

He made no apologies for Marty Howell's drug use or Rachel Moore's prostitution. Quite to the contrary, Kelly maintained, it was their personal wreckage that gave them credibility. This was not, Kelly reminded the jury, a Wall Street case. This was instead a tour of America's domestic Vietnam. A view into the crack infested streets of Queens. To make it understandable, Kelly had to produce the crack soldiers.

"If I had brought in a doctor or a priest, a rabbi or a minister, and told you that he was standing there at 3:30 in the morning on a Thursday night, Friday morning, you legitimately would have had every reason to be somewhat skeptical. But if you take the testimony of all the other witnesses, why isn't it plausible that she would be there at 3:30 in the morning on February 26, 1988? She was a survivor, another person who lives in the world of the Bebos." Kelly said.

Kelly kept discussing the credibility of the witnesses, but the jurors were losing interest. They'd heard enough of Rachel and Arjune and Howell and Newby. So he switched up his tactics. He focused on the Bebos and Pappy Mason and the power the drug dealers held in the hood.

"These people had great, great power. They had the power to hire workers, the power to sell drugs, the power to distribute drugs. This is an awesome power. Ladies and gentlemen of the jury, on the morning of February 26, 1988, these individuals decided to reach an even greater power, a power almost Godlike. It was a power, ladies and gentlemen, over the life and death of another human being. On the morning of February 26, 1988 these individuals exercised that power. The results are what we are here for today."

With all the pomp and hoopla of a statesman, the prosecutor

delivered his case, but there was another side to the story. "The crazy thing about this was Philip Copeland had an airtight alibi. He was laid up with some stunt in a hotel, had proof and everything. So how did they put him with them?" D says. But the prosecution wasn't buying it.

Kelly hammered home the case against Philip Copeland. "Audette Wills goes out to a hotel she has never been in before, stays with an individual she had never stood over with before, goes to the Kennedy Inn and she is up all night. Miraculously, Philip Copeland is the only one that seems able to sleep. Audette is nervous, she can't sleep.

"Philip falls asleep with his clothes on at 3:30, 4:00 in the morning. Philip Copeland, amazingly, on the biggest night in the history of the Bebos, the preconceived murder of a New York City police officer, and Philip Copeland is not involved. Philip Copeland is sleeping in a hotel room. What, are you kidding?" The prosecutor clearly didn't believe Marshal's alibi.

"I think they got a raw deal. The police scared and manipulated them. They were intimidated so they rolled over and flipped. They didn't flip, they lied. If they didn't make those statements they would have never got convicted. That shit was political, when a police gets killed somebody has to pay for it. I think they got railroaded." D says.

Todd Scott's lawyer made an impassioned plea for leniency and understanding to the jury. "There are no ethics today," he said. "That disturbs us all. And the Todd Scott's, it's not only Todd Scott, there are millions of Todd Scott's. He might have failed, ladies and gentlemen, but there's a lot of failures out there. And maybe you and I could do something about it.

"Maybe, you know, we could be a little more caring about these people. And I don't want you to feel any sympathy for the Todd Scott's of this world. But I ask you to consider where they're coming from. And I ask you not to close the door on the Todd Scott's of the world, because the Todd Scott's are going to be out there. They're our generation; they're our youth, our children." The appeal for sympathy didn't work.

With explosive applause by the victim's family and several dozen police officers, the defendants were found guilty of being part of a four man team that cut down rookie officer Edward Byrne. All four men- Todd Scott, David McClary, Philip Copeland, and Scott Cobb- were convicted of "acting in concert" in the murder. The convicted men faced sentences of 25-to-life in prison.

Lawyers for the four men said they would appeal, holding that the trial had been "political" and that Justice Thomas Demakos, the presiding judge, had improperly favored the prosecution in his major rulings. But the mainstream media towed the line. *Jury Convicts all Four Defendants in Queens Murder of Officer Byrne, The New York Times* headline read.

Law enforcement officials considered the slaying, in the words of a prosecutor at the trial, a "declaration of war against our society." The cop killing led to major new drives by police against narcotic traffickers across the city. Squads of undercover officers were assigned to sweep dealers off the streets in South Jamaica's drug plagued neighborhoods. It was a proactive initiative, but to the convicted none of that mattered.

"I'll be back!" Copeland and Scott declared at separate times as they were led back to jail from the courtroom in State Supreme Court in Kew Gardens, after the verdicts were announced. The jury, six men and six women, had deliberated a day and a half after a two month trial.

Scott Cobb, after showing no immediate reaction, muttered an obscenity after the verdict was announced. Officer Byrne's parents, Matthew and Ann, hugged and kissed in the spectator section while other members of the family threw their fists into the air triumphantly and joined the exultant roar of Officer Byrne's colleagues.

Tears welled in Ann Byrne's eyes and Matthew was breathing heavily by the time the final guilty verdicts were announced. He told reporters that the verdicts were, "A message from society back to the mutts," and that while the convictions, "Are not going to bring Eddie back, hopefully these verdicts will make this city safer."

Queens District Attorney John Santucci, who prosecuted the case, said the outcome showed that "you can't go to war and kill a cop." Defense lawyers countered the conviction, contending that the most important prosecution witnesses were unreliable and unsavory people who had made deals to escape prosecution for their own crimes or were interested in the $130,000 reward money offered in the case.

But the defendants cut their own throats with the videotaped confessions they made right after their arrests. The judge and jury had no choice but to find them guilty. By breaking weak under police pressure they told on themselves and kept the investigation going.

250 Cheer as Byrne Killers get 25 Years to Life in Jail, The New York Times headline read on May 17, 1989. At sentencing the Judge declared the defendants were, "Unfit for society. That was an assassination," Justice Demakos said. "A deliberate, premeditated, intentional act to kill a cop. 'For every one of us you take, we'll take one of yours.' This vile act was also a deadly declaration of war against the very foundations of our society and a defilement of the cornerstone on which our criminal justice system is based.

"A cop on duty, guarding a witness to a drug transaction was executed. This arrogant act assaults our society and in turn affects each and every one of us, each and every neighborhood in our city. First we see how witnesses are stalked and killed in these drug infected areas, then a cop is brutally assassinated. Who will be next? Prosecutors and lawyers? Perhaps a judge? In this same city, a Supreme Court Judge has had to have 24 hour police guard because he had the audacity to sentence a drug lord to prison.

"Philip Copeland was convicted of the homicide of Patrolman Byrne, along with Todd Scott, David McClary and Scott Cobb. There is no doubt, that of the three, Copeland was the worst. He was the lieutenant in charge while the drug lord was in prison. The order to 'ice a cop' was transmitted to him, not to those of lesser importance. And, Copeland, you carried out your order to completion. In doing so, you have demonstrated that you are unfit to be a member of our society. I have received a multitude of letters asking that I impose a life sentence without parole. Under the law, I cannot do that.

"However, what I can do and will do, is promise you that I intend to make a recommendation to the Parole Board that you are never paroled. I know I will no longer be sitting on the bench in 25 years, but rest assured, my last judicial function before I retire from the judiciary will be to write the Parole Board to remind them of my strong feeling that I have expressed to you today. The sentence of this court shall be 25-years-to-life with a recommendation to the Parole Board that you never be paroled."

Marshal didn't even blink as the sentence was announced. The cops began to applaud, Matthew Byrne clapping the loudest. Marshal turned and smiled as he was led away. On the way out of court Todd Scott turned to the police and grabbed his crotch. Two hundred and fifty officers cheered at his antics. Ever defiant, the convicted killers were off to prison.

"Bye-bye," yelled one cop. "Have a nice life." Marshal's lawyer, Frank Hancock said that he would appeal the sentence. He also told the judge that his client, a member of the Rastafarian sect, wanted to be assured that his dreadlocks would not be cut in prison and that he would be allowed to "refrain from a meat diet." The lawyer also cited a letter he said he received from a cousin of Copeland, who was an inmate in a state prison and who wrote that he had heard Copeland was in danger of being beaten by state prison guards. Mr. Hancock's statement that there were, "people upstate waiting to victimize Philip Copeland" drew applause from the police officers filling the courtroom.

All four of the convicted men were sentenced to 25-to-life by the state for the cop killing, but the feds were lurking in the background, ready to build a new case, that the orders to execute the cop came from Fat Cat and Pappy Mason. The feds wanted the whole crew to burn for the officer's murder.

Fat Cat's lieutenant Mike Bones believed that Pappy had come to see himself as invincible. "The killing of the cop was more about Pap's ego than anything else," Mike Bones said. "Cat played the game like a grand wizard. Everything he did was thought through. With Pap, it was the opposite. He went on feeling, regardless of the consequences."

It was reported in *The New York Times* that Todd Scott was negotiating a deal with the feds. Charles Rose, the federal prosecutor offered Todd Scott a deal. In making his racketeering case against Fat Cat and Pappy, Rose had already given deals to Viola Nichols and Brain "Glaze" Gibbs. "I confessed to six murders and two attempted murders. Some of them I got paid 20k to do. Fat Cat paid me." Glaze said.

Todd Scott's lawyer told reporters, "The government's offer is really quite wonderful. I wonder if they will give us medical benefits too." It was reported by media outlets that the NYPD and state law enforcement agencies were furious with the feds for offering a cop killer a deal. But that was how the feds got their man. Nobody was too dirty for them to get into bed with.

Todd Scott's lawyer explained how he put it to Todd. "I said, 'Todd, you may think these people are important, but they are not.' I knew by then that there were a lot of rats in the federal case. So I figured if everyone is going to rat everyone else out, I said the person that gets there first gets the bargains."

Todd Scott made a confession in the case on May 12, 1989. This is what he told the U.S. Attorney. "Pappy ordered the hit," Todd Scott said. "Phil saw me in the project and said that Pappy wanted to talk to us. We went to Viola's house on February 24, 1988. We got there at 6:30 p.m. Pappy was talking to Phil on the phone. Present were me, Dave, Phil and Scott Cobb. Pappy talked to Phil only. How did I know who was calling? Viola said it was Pappy.

"He kept calling. Viola picked up the phone and said, 'Phil and Todd is here.' They talked for about an hour. I was watching TV, sitting on the bed. The phone has a long cord. Phil was sitting on the edge of the couch behind the TV. Scott Cobb was in the living room. Viola wouldn't let him in the room. The kid named Housecat was in the bedroom. Dave was at Fiesta's Diner by then. Viola was standing in the living room doorway.

"Phil said we had to see Pappy. He said it to me but loud enough for all to hear. I was told to have Dave and Scott around the next day. No other instructions. I had given Phil money for Pappy's lawyer. We left there together, me and Scott. Phil went his own way. We went back to the projects to my uncle's house.

"That night I left and went to the Kennedy Motor Inn. I registered under an assumed name. I don't recall the name any more. I stayed there the whole night. In the morning I went to check on Pappy's workers. I met Scott at his house. We were just riding around all day in my yellow Chrysler. We were driving around and I saw Dave at Fiesta's. I told him to meet me at 7 o'clock on February 25, 1988.

"Me and Scott went to Lucille's to get food and then to my uncle's house. Got there at 6:30 p.m. Phil came and took me into my room. He had someone with him, a Jamaican guy. I was not introduced. Scott Cobb was in the dining room. Phil showed me a ring he got from Pappy. It was a big ring with a flat surface. It had a Round Table on it. The ring had two P's on one side and a map of Africa on the other. Phil said Pappy had given it to him and told about the police officer.

"Pappy said he wanted a police officer to get hit because he was mad over his conviction. He wanted to show the police officer he was still strong. He said, 'I want Todd to do it.' I said, 'No,' because I was closest to Pappy. I work for Pappy. Dave works for Fat Cat. I told him to get somebody else. Phil decided to let Dave do it because he was new.

"We all left down the elevator and I went to meet Dave and told him what had happened at my uncle's house. I was with Scott. At first, Dave wasn't around. We finally met him at a Kentucky Fried Chicken. I told him, 'They want you to hit a cop.' He goes, 'Why me?'

"Then Phil and Dave was talking about it. Dave said, 'I'll do it.' We dropped Dave off on the evening of the 25th. Scott and I were driving around. We went to my uncle's house looking at movies. Scott came and got me about 2:30 a.m. on the morning of February 26th in my car. It was planned for Scott to come and get me. We went to get Dave.

"We went to Fiesta's. Dave wasn't there. We went to get Dave at his house. We stopped off at my father's house, I saw my father. Then we went to Austin's bar across the street. They went in and I went to talk to my sister. We came back out and Dave said he got something to do. I didn't know whether he had a gun on him. Scott was driving. I was in the backseat lying down. Dave was in the front passenger seat. Phil was with a girl, no one spoke with Copeland that night.

"We were going to the city. We made a u-turn on Remington, Dave said go back to 107th. We both got out, we're around the corner, we couldn't see the police car from where we was at. Another police car pulled up, a marked car with two white guys in it. They talked to Byrne's car, gave him coffee or something.

"Dave was on the other side of the street. He was in the bushes on the side of Byrne's car about one block away. Scott could not see us. He didn't know what was going on. He didn't know because I didn't trust him too much. After the cop car come and shine a light on me, we started walking up the block parallel. I realized what was going to happen.

"I figured Dave had a gun. He came up from the back and I was like, 12 feet away on the driver's side of the street. Dave ran up on him, he had both hands on the gun. He crosses the back of the car, the window is not down. I think the light was on. Byrne didn't see him coming. He had his head down like he was reading. He didn't never see what happened. I am 12 feet away, closest.

"I didn't see him pull the gun the first time. I didn't see him pull the gun. He fired five shots. I heard them. I know he shot a .357 revolver, a big chrome gun. No one said anything when we got back to the car. We never spoke. Scott had the music on, he couldn't hear no shots. Scott wanted to know why he wasn't going to the city, but no one answered.

"Dave took the gun with him. He told me about the .38 caliber ammo the next day. We got arrested, but wasn't all in jail together. I spoke with Pappy on the phone. He asked me why I talk and I said cause I was scared. We had a correction's officer on the switchboard who worked for us. She would patch us all in together so we could talk. Me, Pappy, Dave and Phil. We talked all during the trial. I didn't get piss for doing this. I wanted nothing to do with it."

In the end both Todd Scott and Scott Cobb turned down the chance to cut a deal with the feds. They had momentary lapses of weakness unforgivable in the eyes of the streets, but in the end they took the state to trial and didn't cut any deals with the feds. But their statements were damning to both themselves, Fat Cat and Pappy. It might not have been their intention, but they should have kept their mouths shut.

Cause and effect, a lot of shit went down because of the Edward Byrne cop killing. On that fateful night events were set into motion that would forever change national policy on drugs and the lives of Queens residents. Other legacies would come into play as dudes did what they thought they had to do, just as the feds did what they thought they had to do.

The New York City Police Department formed and introduced the Tactical Narcotics Team, better known as TNT, which would perform military-like operations and sweep Queens clean of the hustlers, drug dealers and denizens of the block. It was a drastic reaction that didn't cure the underlying problem.

Congress would declare the War on Drugs and enact the federal sentencing guidelines and mandatory minimums. Crack dealers would be arrested by the thousands, hundreds of thousands and given 10 year mandatory minimum terms in prison for a couple of rocks. Thrown into the federal system, as the Bureau of Prisons went on a crazy building spree, the likes of which have never been seen, turning the United States into incarceration nation.

"They got a hard on for us because of what happened to Byrne." Shocker says. "They knew I was Bebo so I am guilty by association. They know I was part of that crew and I stood up like a man." But not everyone on the federal indictment, who was a part of Cat's or Pappy's crew stood up.

The indictment charged that between February 1988 and August 11, 1988, the crew conspired with intent to distribute in excess of 50 grams of cocaine base. By virtue of overlapping personnel, mutually beneficial drug transactions and the friendly relationship between Fat Cat and Pappy, both organizations were closely linked and operated together in a cooperative setting. Because of this cooperation, these two organizations were able to establish dominant control; both organizations would often use violent means to insure payment by debtors, to intimidate competitors and to retaliate against law enforcement officers. The jobs were parceled out to whoever was available to accomplish them.

The investigation revealed that there were well over 40 individuals who were regular members of both the Nichols and Mason organizations. These individuals participated in all phases of the illegal drug industry including procuring, processing and distributing various forms of narcotics. Some individuals were also responsible for collecting and disbursing the organization's cash proceeds, while other conducted enforcement related activities.

During the course of the investigation, Char "Shocker" Davis was identified as a member of the Mason organization. It was revealed that between June 1988 and August 11, 1988, he was responsible for the delivery of large amounts of cocaine and crack to fellow organization member Viola Nichols. Under Shocker's direction, it was Viola's job to break down and package the drugs into bags or vials worth approximately $5 a piece on the street.

Following the drugs being packaged, they would be returned to Shocker, or his underling Ryan "Ninja" Pelt, and then distributed among several street level dealers who were also under the control of Shocker. Then after the drugs were sold, the dealers would deliver cash proceeds to Shocker who in turn would give the cash to Paris "Mimi" Williams, who served in essence as the crew's bookkeeper.

Based on testimony from C.I.'s between early June and

July 1988, Shocker was responsible for delivering almost 1000 grams of crack cocaine a week to Viola Nichols for packaging. Shocker was also responsible for the delivery of additional drugs to as many as four other individuals in the organization, who had packaging responsibilities similar to that of Viola Nichols. It should be noted that by virtue of his position in the Mason organization, Shocker was aware and possibly even responsible for many of the crew's act of violence.

In the electronically monitored telephone calls the feds were tracking, Shocker mentioned the beating and subsequent hospitalization of an individual, who reportedly robbed one of the crew's street level dealers. During the conversation Shocker stated that the beating was conducted by fellow Bebo, David "Hammer" Robinson.

Shocker also spoke of being wanted by the police for questioning in a homicide of a young woman believed to be killed by fellow Bebos Todd Scott and Philip Copeland. Shocker also stated that he was wanted for the murder of another young woman, only identified as Michelle. To the feds, Cat's crew and the Bebos were violence incarnate. Shocker disagrees.

"First time they came to me with that body was right after I blew trial." He says. "My lawyer told me Ms. Caldwell wanted me to look at some pictures. She showed me two photos of dead bodies. One was Misha, who Fat Cat said he ordered killed because she was cheating. They showed me her picture and the picture of this dude Bellamy and asked if I knew anything about it.

"I told Ms. Caldwell she could suck my dick. Then a week later they materialized a body, Charlene's, and said I did it. They said Viola told them I told her about it. But that's bullshit. They had a phone conversation where I told Viola that I was gonna lay low for a minute because some homicide cops came around to question me and they ran with it." It wasn't the only thing the feds would run with.

CHAPTER 8

Betrayal

As a youth all I ever did was sell crack/ I used to idolize Cat/Hurt me in my heart to hear that nigga snitched on Pap/How he go out like that. **50 Cent, Ghetto Qu'ran, Guess Who's Back (2002)**

With everyone in jail and the block completely shut down, tensions among the crew were high. Fat Cat was looking for a way to get his mother and female relatives out of jail. It was the least he could do. Fat Cat had resigned himself to spending the rest of his life in prison. He figured there was no hope for him. With a litany of cases before him, he could see the writing on the wall and his odds did not look good.

It's said he sent word from prison through lieutenants like Joseph "Bobo" Rogers, aka Mike Bones that he didn't mind if female family members such as Viola testified against him in order to receive a reduced prison sentence. An honorable thing to do for his family and loved ones, but one that opened up doors for Cat's enemies and detractors to twist his actions any which way they could. Cat was looking out for the hood team, but the streets could construe it any way they wanted.

Pappy was in no mood for self-sacrifice, even if his mother faced a lengthy prison sentence. "I couldn't believe Pappy was gonna let his mother go to trial," Mike Bones said. "I said 'Pap, how you gonna do that? How you gonna let your mom go to trial?'" Pappy was resolute, he would hold to the "G" code, despite his mother.

To worsen things for the crew, Pappy started bucking and wilding at MCC New York in Manhattan, the federal holding facility, threatening guards and reinforcing the image of Fat Cat's crew as cop killers and gun thugs just as they were about to go to trial. It was behavior some dudes in the crew couldn't abide. They were sick of Pappy and his antics.

Mike Bones told Pappy to chill the fuck out and Pappy took offense, sending him a threat through his little soldier Shocker. "Pap said I'd better be ready," Mike Bones said. "I told Shocker, 'Cut off your dreads, put them in an envelope and give them to Pap.'" Shocker didn't cut off shit and he let Pappy know what Mike Bones said. The beef between crew members was on.

Pappy made his move during an attorney visit when all the codefendants were gathered in a strategy meeting for the upcoming trial. Pappy showed up in war gear, his prison jumpsuit stuffed with magazines to protect him from shank attacks. He also had a shank with Mike Bones name on it. Mike Bones was ready to go also. He had a rope tied around his hand attached to a shank.

"I wrapped the rope around my wrist and when Pap passed by I grabbed him by his dreads and stabbed him." Mike Bones said. Pappy stabbed back and Mike Bones wrestled Pappy to the ground, getting stabbed in the process. A crowd gathered until Fat Cat got up and separated the men, he told them both to chill, not to fight and that the feds were the enemy.

Cat didn't want any fights between the crew members, so the beef was dead. The sides still splintered and divided into factions, no matter what Cat said. The lines in the sand had been clearly drawn and instead of standing united, the crews fractured. Despite the Cat's best intentions, when his crew should have been unified, they were at each other's throats.

"I saw Pappy every day." Shocker says. "They had him and Fat Cat behind the glass in the hole at MCC. Fat Cat had a little more freedom. Pap was in high security. The only time he could get out of his cell was when they gave him recreation one hour a day or to take a shower. The only time he got out was when I came once in the morning and once in the evening for the codefendant meetings.

"He used to be able to go down on the third floor with all the codefendants to see their attorneys, but Pap's girlfriend, Vanessa, God bless the dead, came to see somebody and Pap went off on her, saying why you violating and spit in her face so he couldn't go on the third floor anymore." As the pressure mounted the feds came with their copouts.

"The feds offered me and Pap and maybe two other guys 40 years under the old law to cop out to an 848 in exchange for our mother's freedom. Pap said he wasn't going to plead guilty to something he didn't do and he went to bat with them. I took the plea." Cat said. A lot of others on the case took pleas, but Pappy and a few of the rest like Shocker, mostly the diehard Bebos, went to trial.

"Mostly all the females got phone counts. They copped out to phone counts." Shocker says. They were doing as Fat Cat instructed, letting the weight fall on him. But the streets called them snitches. "Pap said fuck that, he was always going to fight till the end. Pap stood his ground, but Cat thought about his mom," the Queens hustler said.

On July 27, 1989, following a jury trial Char "Shocker" Davis was found guilty and sentenced to 405 months. "Pap's mom went to trial with me," Shocker says. *Pappy Mason's Mother Gets 10 Year Term, The New York Times* headline read. Officers who raided her home in the Crown Heights section of Brooklyn found more than two pounds of crack and during her trial prosecutors played recordings of intercepted telephone calls of Mrs. Mason discussing her illegal drug operation.

"Did her eight years and went home. She stood up. Pap's

girl mysteriously left a package of crack in his mom's house the day before the feds raided. Pap's mom didn't do nothing wrong. Mimi claimed she was on her way to the club and was gonna go back and get the package of crack, but she didn't. The feds, they don't play fair." Shocker said. With all the pleas and people cooperating, superseding indictments were being handed down and Pappy's name was on them.

On August 24, 1989, *The New York Times* headline read, *Drug Gang Chief Charged in Officers Killing.* Pappy was indicted on ordering the murder of Edward Byrne. It was a long time coming, and finally the feds put the indictment together and charged him. The 11 count indictment included five counts of narcotics trafficking and two counts of using juveniles to traffic in drugs.

"We are satisfied that we have accounted for all those responsible for the murder of Officer Byrne," Andrew Maloney, the U.S. Attorney for the Eastern District of New York said. "With this indictment we are putting away one of the most vicious monsters in the drug trade today." Pappy was made out to be a villain of the highest order by the government. A drug thug of epic proportions.

Mr. Maloney said reports that Officer Byrne was not singled out as the victim appeared to be correct. "It could have been any police officer sitting in that car. Pappy Mason had just had an altercation with another cop on the street that cost him face and his organization was getting hurt by the anti-narcotics drive. He was being treated with disrespect and he could not accept that." Mr. Maloney finished.

Mr. Maloney said the drug sweep and arrest of more than 30 narcotic traffickers in Queens, electronic surveillance and evidence developed for the earlier trials in State Supreme Court in Queens, provided the information that led to the murder indictment against Pappy Mason. He said the members of Mason's gang, known as the Bebos, were fiercely loyal to their leader, who they regarded "with almost cult like awe."

He said they received their orders from Pappy in coded

conversations over jailhouse telephones and in prison visits. To circumvent police surveillance, the gang members would "talk Jamaican." Scott Cobb told police "the message" behind the slaying of Officer Byrne was that, "We lose one, they lose one" and that, "The show don't stop," despite the arrests of top drug dealers.

For the respected and feared Fat Cat, things started to get a bit shady. On September 30, 1989 *The New York Times* headline read, *Queens Drug Kingpin Reportedly Pleads Guilty.* The paper reported that in an unusual secret court proceeding, Lorenzo Nichols pled guilty to two federal racketeering related murder charges and started cooperating with investigators.

The paper said that Fat Cat was providing information about Pappy Mason. "You might say that the Fat Cat has turned into a canary," one law enforcement official said. "Because of his cooperation, he'll be able to realize his dream of coming home to his grandchildren."

Another official said that Mr. Nichols was providing information about former associates in his drug ring, as well as those in other organizations. He said that Fat Cat would testify against Pappy and others. The official, who did not want to be identified, said that Mr. Nichols was hoping that his cooperation might lead the federal judge who accepted the guilty plea to give him a shorter prison term than the life sentence without possibility of parole, carried by the homicide counts specified in the racketeering charge.

The homicide counts included those of a former girlfriend and a drug rival, authorities said. But even if Fat Cat cooperated fully, they said, he faced a very long federal prison sentence, on top of his state time. They said he probably had other reasons for cooperating, including a hope that his mother, Louise Coleman and his girlfriend, Karolyn Tyson, would receive more lenient treatment by the government.

Wearing an orange colored jumpsuit, Fat Cat was transported under tight security from FCI Ottisville, a federal prison in upstate New York to the basement garage of the U.S. Courthouse in downtown Brooklyn. From the garage, he was taken by a special elevator to the fourth floor chambers of Judge Edward Korman. Pleadings were normally listed in the court calendar and carried out in open court, but Fat Cat's session was unannounced and closed. The record of the proceedings was placed under seal by the court. The feds didn't want Cat's business getting out to the public.

"Sealed pleas are extraordinary measures taken by the government," U.S. Attorney Maloney said. "And are usually done for investigative or life threatening reasons." Robert Simels, Fat Cat's popular guns-and-drugs lawyer, who was abruptly replaced, said he didn't know if his former client was cooperating.

"He never said he wanted to cooperate with the government." But he added that Mr. Nichols had been very concerned about his mother and his girlfriend. "He wanted them to receive probation or light sentences."

Simels had been replaced as Fat Cat's lawyer without advance notice and under "very strange circumstances." He did not understand how Mr. Nichols had qualified as an indigent defendant. But he went on, "It makes sense if a deal was being made for him to cooperate." Simels was known for winning cases against the government and if the Cat was switching teams he didn't need the high-priced lawyer.

The extent of Fat Cat's cooperation or if he cooperated at all has never been known. He denies it, as do many members of his former crew, who in all reality are the ones who matter. No one has produced paperwork that Fat Cat testified against them. But the newspapers reported the proceedings and news of the secret court sessions quickly spread on the streets of Queens and in law enforcement circles sparking much talk and debate.

The agreement of Cat to testify against his underling Pappy Mason or testify down as it is called, infuriated members of the state law enforcement community. "Using Fat Cat to get Pappy is like using syphilis to get gonorrhea," one cop said. But that was how the feds operated.

On October 1, 1989, Fat Cat's 72-year-old mother, Louis

Coleman was allowed to plead guilty to reduced charges. Although Coleman had originally faced life in prison, she was given probation. "I ain't did nothing," Coleman said. "I was always working. I ain't never had no drugs in my hand in my life."

This was the same woman who had been captured on a secret tape recording, warning an associate, "Don't come in the store front no more. I don't care no more if I put two bullets in your head." It seems that Cat's mama was gangster for real.

The New York Times headline read *Drug Boss Tells of Giving order to Kill My Girl,* on October 5, 1989. In his secret pleading, the newspaper reported that Cat had his former girlfriend, Myrtle "Misha" Horsheim, the mother of Cat's five-year-old son, killed because she stole money from him and spent it on a dude.

Judge Korman asked Fat Cat, "Was one of the purposes of this to teach other people in the organization a lesson about not stealing from you?" The Cat replied, "It wasn't just stealing. It was the fact that she was my girl and that she took my money and spent it on another person. She made me look bad in front of people who was within the organization." The murder took place in December 1987.

Fat Cat also told the judge how he had ordered the murder in November 1986 of a drug rival Isaac Bolden. He told Judge Korman that Bolden and others had robbed people in his organization. "I known him for years and so I told him, 'Just don't worry about what you did. Just go ahead and point me towards the people that was with you.' And he did that, he pointed me toward the people that was with him. And then he turned around and point the people toward me."

At the request of federal prosecutors, the proceedings in the judge's chamber, as well as the plea agreement were sealed by the court. But prosecutors had the material unsealed after several reporters said they would seek to have the papers made public. U.S. Attorney Andrew Maloney said his office had wanted the information kept secret for investigative and security reasons. He said it was made public after it was widely disclosed in the press that Fat Cat was cooperating.

Mr. Maloney said that if Nichols cooperated fully, Judge Korman could take that into consideration. "His only chance of getting less than mandatory life is if the judge finds that he did something extraordinary," the U.S. Attorney said. Fat Cat pled guilty to two counts of committing violent crimes, namely murder, in aid of racketeering. Both counts carried maximum penalties of life.

In the plea agreement it was written that, "Lorenzo Nichols will cooperate fully with this office, the FBI, the NYPD and other law enforcement agencies as this office may require. Lorenzo Nichols agrees to be fully debriefed concerning his knowledge of and participation in, any criminal activity, included but not limited to, narcotics trafficking and homicide, Lorenzo Nichols agrees to testify at any proceedings in this District and any other District.

"Lorenzo Nichols must at all times give complete, truthful and accurate information and testimony. Should it be judged by this office that Lorenzo Nichols has intentionally given false, misleading or incomplete information or testimony, has failed to cooperate fully or has otherwise violated any provision of this agreement, Lorenzo Nichols may be deemed, at this office's election, to have breached this agreement.

"Lorenzo Nichols must not commit, nor attempt to commit any further crimes. In the event that Lorenzo Nichols does commit or attempts to commit any further crimes, this office will deem this agreement null and void. If this office determines that Lorenzo Nichols has made a good faith effort to provide substantial assistance to law enforcement, this office, pursuant to section 5kl.1 of the sentencing guidelines will file a motion with the sentencing court in the Eastern District of New York setting forth the nature and extent of his cooperation with this office.

"If Lorenzo Nichols requests and in this office's judgment that the request is reasonable, this office will make application and recommend that he be placed in the Witness Security program." The plea agreement was signed on September 28, 1989 by Fat

Cat, his lawyer Lawrence Vogelman and Assistant U.S. Attorney Leslie Caldwell. Fat Cat entered the Witness Protection program in 1990.

Pappy Mason went to trial alone in the federal racketeering case. Pappy boycotted most of his own trial, preferring to follow the proceedings on a specially installed speaker system in his cell. Pap was so violent in court that the U.S. Marshals had to isolate him. "They did me wrong," Pappy said. "Jah is God, it was no trial at all, it was a KKK meeting for real." Pap's vehemence toward the government was legendary.

"I refused to cooperate even though my mother faced jail time." Pappy said. "She knows about white people. She said God will make a way. I'm not letting these crackers roll me. I am strong; I will never give up on Bebo. I'm the hip-hop kid from Southside Queens."

At Pappy's federal trial, Scott Cobb was a surprise witness. He testified that Marshal told him, "Pappy wanted a police officer killed," because the police "disrespected him." A lot of so-called soldiers rolled on Pappy Mason, one reason his legacy is so strong today. Under the most trying circumstances and with seemingly the whole world against him Pappy held strong.

There was also a mention of a possible killing of a second officer. The judge said it was "chatter among co-conspirators" but Mike Bones brought it up to prosecutors. A lot of the players in Cat's crew ended up turning on Pappy Mason, as they blamed him for the mess they were in. They were getting revenge on Pappy the only way they could, by flipping the script and testifying against him..

Mike Bones was originally Pappy's codefendant, but he pled guilty to drug conspiracy charges and cooperated with prosecutors. Mike Bones told the jury that he operated his own drug business, served as lieutenant to Cat and did favors for Pappy. Under cross examination Pappy's court appointed lawyer, Harry Batchelder, got Mike Bones to acknowledge that he had been involved in three homicides and one attempted homicide. Under his plea agreement, he testified, he would not be prosecuted.

With Pappy staring at him from the defense table, Mike Bones testified that, "Pappy wanted another cop killed to show the cops he ain't playing." Pappy rose from the defense table and said in a low voice, "I'm leaving." But Judge Korman persuaded Pappy it was in his best interest to stay and assist his lawyer. Pappy had refused to attend earlier court sessions.

Officials said Mason had a nervous breakdown and had to be treated at FMC Springfield, a federal prison hospital in Missouri. Harry Batchelder, Pappy's lawyer, tried to enter an insanity defense at the November 1989 trial. But the judge wasn't going for it.

Pappy's lawyer tried to convince the judge that his client was not mentally fit to assist in his own defense. He said his client tried to assault him during a jailhouse visit, would not cooperate with him and had hallucinations and believed that his mother "was performing voodoo exercises on his head." But after hearing testimony from a prison psychologist, the judge said he found Pappy to be "rational and lucid" and allowed the trial to continue.

"Pappy Mason's burnt out." The Queens hustler says. "I was with him at MCC in 92. He had dreads down to the floor, slept underneath the bed and smoked a carton of cigs a day. They said he was bugged out. That he was crazy, but that don't take nothing away from him. Street niggas love this dude because they know he gets busy." But the feds were busy trying to bury Pappy.

"Cat's sister Viola Nichols and Joseph 'Mike Bones' Rogers pointed their fingers at Pap and testified at his federal trial." Prince said. And they weren't the only ones to betray their former comrade according to Prince.

"Fat Cat and Mike Bones worked together to place murders on others, especially Pappy Mason. When Cat tried to reach out to me for assistance in any way, I'd turn my back because I didn't trust him. Pap knew I never trusted Cat. Many times we discussed the rumors circulating about Cat in the state prison system regarding him making statements on a guy named Barsun concerning a homicide."

Viola Nichols spent three days on the stand, saying she

would say anything to protect her brother Fat Cat. She testified that Pappy Mason ordered a policeman slain because another officer had embarrassed him in front of members of his drug gang. She said that shortly after Officer Edward Byrne was slain she told Pappy that her brother was angered by the killing. Pappy telephoned Viola the day after the cop killing and told her, "Oh, yeah, that's the way it goes. They get one of ours. We get one of theirs." *Witness says Revenge Led to Officer's Killing, The New York Times* reported.

Viola Nichols testified that the day after the slaying the four men who carried out the murder came to her home and were there when Pappy called from the Brooklyn House of Detention. Scott Cobb, referring to the telephone call, said that Marshal told them after speaking to Pappy that, "Pappy said that we had done a good job, that it had gone down real smooth."

Viola was in tears in her role as the prime witness, admitting that she was a drug addict and a thief willing to lie to avoid death or injury. She confessed under cross examination to violations of her plea agreement with prosecutors and using her government stipend to buy crack. Viola admitted to committing at least seven felonies involving drugs and had lied to at least one jury. She also admitted credit card fraud, fake check schemes and tax and welfare fraud. Fat Cat was never called to the stand.

The jury deliberated for three days before finding Pappy guilty of ordering the Byrne murder. He watched the verdict over a closed circuit television which had replaced his speaker in a detention cell in the United States Courthouse in Brooklyn. To Pappy it was all just some KKK bullshit.

"He showed no emotion, he didn't even blink," a U.S. Marshal said about Pappy when he saw the verdict. There was a gasp of apparent relief from many in the packed courtroom when the jury announced the verdict on the last count, the murder charge. Matthew Byrne was seen weeping, his bowed head resting on folded arms.

"Today's conviction accounts for all the people who had a hand in the brutal murder of Police Officer Byrne," the U.S.

Attorney said. In her closing arguments to the jury, Leslie Caldwell said that Mason felt the police- by putting him in jail and in other ways- had "disrespected" him in front of his workers. She added that Mason feared the "loss of respect" would lead to a "loss of power" and ultimately a "loss of control" over his drug operation.

Steven O'Day, the juror who read the verdict, said the jury quickly reached a unanimous decision on the 11 counts in the indictment. "In our minds, we knew we would be doing the right thing in convicting him." Mr. O'Day said. "But we were wondering whether there was enough evidence and we spent a lot of time deliberating." After reviewing all the evidence, he said, everyone became convinced of Pappy's guilt on the murder charge.

Pappy's lawyer said the government's case depended on "hearsay" from convicted criminals and admitted liars who would "sing the French national anthem backwards to save their skins." Cooperator testimony is the norm in most federal organized crime trials. Without the conspiracy charges and cooperation the feds wouldn't have a 98 percent conviction rate.

Before being sentenced, Pappy was transferred to FMC Butler, a federal prison medical center in North Carolina, for extensive psychiatric tests. Dr. Daniel Schwartz, a director of forensic psychiatry at King's County Hospital testified that Mason was "unfit to be sentenced" and appeared to have a transient mental ailment, probably caused by stress.

Pappy's lawyer said he would wait for the results of the new psychiatric examination before deciding whether to have his client declared incompetent and ask for a new trial. *The New York Times* headline read, *Convicted Drug Leader 'Unfit to be Sentenced.'* It took several years but finally the courts cleared Pappy to be sentenced.

On January 9, 1994, Pappy Mason was sentenced to life. In a bizarre proceeding, in which Pappy periodically dropped to the floor to do pushups before the bench, he ranted, cursed and threatened to kill the judge and the prosecutor, Leslie Caldwell.

His lawyers argued he was unfit to be sentenced, but the judge wasn't swayed.

"I believe he is competent to be sentenced at this time," Judge Korman said. Ms. Caldwell said that when Pappy dropped to the floor in front of the judges bench to do his pushups, which he repeated "15 or 20" times the federal Marshals guarding him did not try to stop him.

His lawyer told the judge, "He speaks with a rush of words that just don't belong there, a wind of words that come out and don't add up too much." Between his sets of pushups, Pappy stood quietly next to his lawyer, his dreadlocks in a ponytail that extended below his belt.

On Pappy's life sentence Leslie Caldwell said, "There is no reason to think that anything other than keeping him in prison will deter him from committing violent, vicious crimes like the ones he's already committed. This is the only kind of sentence that will protect society from this defendant." *Drug Dealer is Sentenced to Life for Ordering Killing of Officer, The New York Times* declared.

Fat Cat and Pappy's demise was national news, as was the fallen officer, who became a national hero in death. "We salute Eddie Byrne. We salute his family for their determination that his death will not have been in vain." President Reagan said.

In January 1989, the secret informer Billy Martin was removed from South Jamaica's streets and put into the Witness Protection Program. Six months later he got kicked out. Billy's treatment infuriated city detectives and members of the Queens District Attorney's Office. He had contributed as much as anyone- detective, FBI agent, DEA agent, prosecutor, judge or American President- to creating the massive federal racketeering and narcotics cases that had crushed the murderous crack gangs of South Jamaica.

Billy had worn a radio transmitter in his Yankees cap, carried miniature tape recorders and starred in government surveillance videotapes of huge drug buys. With his help, the feds had nailed drug kingpins Robert "Cornbread" Gray, Fat Cat, Pappy Mason,

Supreme, Claude Skinner and the Corley Brothers. Billy Martin was the Queens super snitch.

In exchange for his help he was to be given 65 grand and new identities for himself, his wife and children. The government reneged on both promises, even as George Bush was announcing an all out drug war to combat crack dealers. It just goes to show how the feds will use a rat up like a whore and then hang them out to dry. Like Arjune, Billy Martin went to the newspapers.

His story headlined, *Out in the Cold*, was front page news in the *New York Daily News*. The government left Billy Martin, its secret informer on the street, a price on his head, wondering why anyone would ever agree to work with the federal government in a drug case. The reality was bone chilling.

"George Bush is walking around with Edward Byrne's badge in his pocket," Martin said. "What is he going to do for me? I was the first person to give the cops the names of Byrne's killers. Now I don't even have a valid driver's license in my name. I don't exist. I'm dead and I don't even know it." The feds didn't care though, Billy Martin was of no use to them anymore, so they discarded him like trash.

Fat Cat was back in the news in 1992. *Queens Drug Dealer Pleads Guilty in 1985 Killing of Parole Officer, The New York Times* headline read. The Cat and law enforcement had settled their accounts. It was a plea that the Queens District Attorney's Office, the family and colleagues of the dead parole officer, Brian Rooney, insisted that Mr. Nichols owed, because even though someone else shot the officer, they were convinced Cat ordered the killing.

Cat was immediately given the maximum sentence allowed of 25-to-life in prison, to run concurrent with his previous 25-to-life in the state, for his drug kingpin conviction. The Cat was also sentenced to 40 years by the feds for his 1989 plea.

The 40 year federal sentence was less than the life term that could have been imposed. The term was reduced because authorities said the Cat had given information to federal investigators about former associates and other traffickers. The federal sentence ran concurrent with the state sentences.

Brian Rooney's brother, John, urged the Judge to give Fat Cat life. "He was murdered for doing his job as a parole officer," John Rooney said. "Do not let the defendant in this case bargain away his accountability. I urge you not to grant the defendant the chance to murder again." Fat Cat insisted to Judge Nicholas Pituro in State Supreme Court that he had not meant for Rooney to be killed. He had told Pappy Mason only "to have Rooney hurt."

At the federal sentencing the Cat appeared with a shaved head, stylish slacks, sweater and expensive crocodile loafers. "There were things I did that I'm not proud of," Cat told Judge Korman. "I was young. I was thinking like a street person. As I got older and thought about human life, my values changed. If I could take them back I would."

Judge Korman justified the 40 year federal sentence by saying that other convictions- including Pappy Mason's for ordering the slaying of the cop- may not have been obtained without Fat Cat's help. The Cat had gone full circle, from respected street general to being credited by the government and papers for his cooperation efforts.

Later that year as the Supreme Team got ready to go to trial against the feds in their own racketeering case, Fat Cat's name emerged in the media again. For publicity purposes the Cat truly did have nine lives. *Turncoat Drug Kingpin To Testify; Fat Cat To Sing About Ex Ally*, the *New York Newsday* headline read on October 1, 1992.

The paper reported that the Cat would reemerge from hiding to testify that Gerald "Prince" Miller arranged assassinations for him while he was in jail. The Cat told the feds that two men, cousins Isaac and Henry Boldin, had stolen more than 100 grand in money and drugs from him and that Prince tracked them down and had them shot at Nichols' request. Isaac Bolden was killed. Henry Bolden survived.

"He did tell on me," Prince said. "What he told was lies. Fat Cat provided information against several individuals.

These brought major attention from law enforcement toward the Supreme Team. Cat led the authorities to believe that I was responsible for numerous homicides. He told them that I assisted him in the killings of his enemies. When in fact he manipulated and used Puerto Rican Righteous to do his bidding behind my back.

"Cat, Mike Bones and Righteous all knew that I was the next big fish the state and federal authorities wanted to hook. When all three of them flipped they pointed their fingers at me for crimes they conspired together to commit without my knowledge. Cat tells the feds that while we were in jail together in the Brooklyn House I expressed my involvement in several crimes, he told the feds these lies to satisfy his cooperation agreement."

CHAPTER 9
Legacy

*I hung around the older crews/While they sling smack
to dingbats/They spoke of Fat Cat, that niggas name
made bell rings, black. Nas, Memory Lane (sittin' in
Da Park) Illmatic (1994)*

In the third decade of his incarceration Cat's name still remains relevant. "He was a major figure that got a lot of paper," BC says. "Believe me when I tell you, 26 years later, if you walk down 150th Street and 107th Avenue, people still remember it as Cat's block.

"Looking back I didn't realize I was coming up in a legendary place that was gonna make dudes rich and their names famous. I'm appreciative that out of mad hoods in New York's five boroughs my hood was able to distinguish itself from the rest. The feds will never allow that block to get established like that ever again because of what Fat Cat brought."

Fat Cat's name has remained iconic in his hood and in hip-hop. "I saw a lot of love and loyalty coming out of Fat Cat's camp toward his son and dude was in the can for six years already." BC says. "In 1991, his son had a little issue with a dude that gets busy on the low. Cat was notified and that situation was settled instantly."

Due to the notoriety and infamy, hip-hop artists such as 50 Cent, Ja Rule, Nas, Fat Joe and Ghostface, have been invoking New York gangsters like Fat Cat for ages. The rappers love the bravado and fearlessness of the crime boss lore. They emulate the styles, attitudes and mentalities of the drug lords.

"It all started in Queens, from the Godfather hats to the big rope chains. Rappers like LL and Run would copy that style and people would emulate them everywhere. The whole bling thing is a progression from the big rope chains. The genesis is right there in Queens." Curtis Scoon said.

"Fat Cat had so much of an impact on the whole game, whether its streets or the entertainment world. The thing about Cat that distinguished him from all the other people who made money, is the activities that went on with his crew, such as the killing of a police officer, people connected to them were accused of that.

"His name and his right hand man, Pappy Mason, their names have been in countless rap songs. Nas, 50, his whole crew, they all reference them. What you see in hip-hop has Queens all over it. When you see the Lost Boyz and the dreadlocks and all that, it's from Pappy Mason. There's so many little things the rappers picked up on from these guys and presented it to the world." Cat and Pappy's influence was tremendous.

"Lorenzo Nichols was truly a king." The Queens hustler says. "They was legends, urban legends from the hood. Can't nobody front on that. I think these guys were living a movie. They were like rock stars. They used to watch *Scarface* and *The Godfather* and they wanted to live that."

The rappers who idolized them, put the street legends in the public eye by dropping their names in verse. The meeting of hip-hop and hustlers was a combustible one. Survival on the streets required realistic, untarnished assessments of hustles and the hustlers who plied their trade on the block, whereas hip-hop thrived on the romantic belief in the outsized urban legend and myths.

While the streets downplayed the criminal aspects in an attempt to maintain an image of legitimacy, hip-hop pushed the envelope, actively courting and portraying the gangster lifestyle. Real hustlers were accustomed to the cruel twists of fate the drug game held, but the rappers portrayed a Teflon Don attitude in their emulation, because they knew they could swagger off the video set at the end of the day. No real consequences involved. They were actors in a three minute movie, free to be whoever they wanted to be.

The story of the Southside of Jamaica Queens was glorified in rap videos, but the reality was never advertised. The true story was that the hustlers always ended up paying for their dominance on the streets, with their lives, or with lifelong prison sentences. No amount of romanticism could glorify that disastrous end result.

New York streets where killers walk/Like Pistol Pete and Pappy Mason/Gave the young boys' admiration, Nas spit on *God's Son*. As Cat's legacy has gone down in infamy, Pappy is still respected to this day as a go hard soldier who lived and breathed the streets. He is held in reverence for observing the street code to the very end. Pappy should have died in a hail of bullets, but even buried in ADX Florence, the Bureau of Prison's supermax, his legend still resonates.

Pappy's a fighter and maintains to this day, "I didn't do it." His name has been kept alive, in hip-hop and the streets, despite being incarcerated for over 20 years. He is a man, a myth and a folk hero to rap music's elite. In the annals of street lore Pappy Mason has stood tall over time as the crazy guy, crazy guys were afraid of. Jay Z, Nas and 50 Cent have lionized him and his exploits in verse, making him an iconic figure.

In *Ghetto Qu'ran* from the *Guess Who's Back* mixtape, 50 Cent rapped, *Go against crews like Bebo and killers like Pap Mason*. On *The World Is Yours*, Nas rhymed that he was *Facin' time like Pappy Mason*. "He was a cool-ass nigga, but he could get violent in a minute. Bug out and all that shit. But still the nigga was cool,"

BC says.

"That nigga took the time. He ain't crying, he took it and he doing it. You got to salute a nigga like that. I just know this nigga is burned out, but Pap's a stand up nigga, they love that nigga, son. They love that nigga because he stood up. He is in the joint and he still don't give a fuck, his influence is so strong a heritage that's not even his own salutes this dude. The Jamaicans claim Pap like he's one of their own. He's not. He's American. He defied the police in the street; he defied them in jail, how real is that? Some niggas don't bend, they don't move, they fight, it's the nature of a nigga like Pap."

Pappy is still fighting to overturn his conviction and life sentence in the feds, waging a constant battle on multiple fronts. "That was not an indictment that was the government." Pap said. "I am not crazy. I am in prison for something I did not do." Pappy is so vicious in prison he'd cut up anyone who was a snitch. Just on G.P.

His time in prison became so turbulent that prison officials admitted they couldn't control him. He became known for throwing piss or shit at the C/O's and waiting for the riot squad to come. He would wage constant guerrilla warfare from his cell in SHU. He'd fight the guards day and night, battling the goon squads and cell extraction teams. Pappy long ago forfeited his right to be on a regular compound.

Pappy would gear up in his war accessories ready to do battle against the prison guards. He'd wrap his head in towels to soften the blows from the riot squad's batons and saturate his upper body with baby oil to prepare for battle with a phalanx of armored and helmeted guards. It was his own private war he was waging against authorities. The feds shot him up with Thorozine in an effort to curtail his violent behavior.

"The government shot me up with Thorozine, but Jah makes a way so God brings me back to Bebo," Pappy said. "One love to my brethen Fat Cat, Supreme, Delroy, Spoon and Ruff. To my man Marshal, keep your head up. Jah is with us, stay strong. To all the Bebos, stay up and stay Bebo."

After 18 years at USP Marion, Pappy was shipped to ADX Florence where he now resides with the who's who of the gangster chronicles - Wayne Perry, Pistol Pete, Anthony Jones, Larry Hoover- the baddest urban gangsters on the planet. And David McClary, the accused shooter in the Edward Byrne murder, now denies that Pappy ever gave him an order to kill a cop.

Fat Cat has taken a different route to fame during his incarceration from the man he is forever linked to. Sporting a cleanly shaved head and gold wire framed spectacles, the Cat has the physique of an NFL running back. He goes by Busy now instead of Fat Cat. "I don't want people to think I changed my name. Biz has always been my name. I just don't like to use Fat Cat anymore cause that's a name I had as a kid. I'm not comfortable with that as a 48-year-old man." Cat said.

On his sentence and time in jail Cat said, "This is jail. If you can't do this you shouldn't be doing crime." Cat is now in the New York state system serving out his multiple 25-to-life terms. "He's fighting to get to population in Clinton and two inmates convicted in the Edward Byrne case expressed fear for their lives to the Warden so he remains in lock up." Curtis Scoon said.

But Cat has only been in the state system for a few years. Most of his time was spent in the federal Witsec Program in the Bureau of Prisons, from 1990 to about 2006 to be exact. "Cat was a serious guy. Not for any games that go on in prison and not real friendly," a former BOP Witsec prisoner who was in the program with Cat says.

"If you were cool with him you were alright. He had his own routine and was a workout nut. In better shape than most pro athletes, but had skin that hangs off his body from being so fat at one time. He was no nonsense, cold and lacked of feelings for anyone other than his kids. He loved his sons.

"He didn't interact with other dudes much. Stayed in the cell when he wasn't working out. Would play basketball every now and then, but sucked and if he thought a guy fouled him too hard it was on. He rarely ate the kitchen food, hit the microwave and back to his cell. No meat, only fish, rice and beans."

With all the infamous dudes in the BOP Witsec Program, Cat was one of the most high profile. He was very aware of his infamy and notoriety. "He knew he was a street legend in New York, the songs he was in," the former Witsec prisoner says.

"Cat said he was blamed for a lot of stuff he had no part of and took a lot of the weight to keep his family out of prison. He would tell some stories, such as when he had his son's mother killed because he felt disrespected by her when he was in prison or when he made a crew member shoot himself in the leg while he was on the phone because the guy didn't do what he was told about placing a large wager on a fight.

"Cat loved the power he had, said the power and control became a drug for him. Talked about a lot of the guys who were out there who snitched on the down low and were playing the keep it real shit, he despised them. You know his oldest son went to state prison in New York for shooting a dude for calling Cat a snitch. Cat talked about the money he made. Still has money and properties, jewelry. He talked about his contacts at Murder Inc. Wished he was there for the real money that the suckers were getting."

Two decades after his heyday, the Cat was in the news again. *Convicted Drug Lord admits Role in Stealing Luxury Automobiles*, *The Associate Press* reported on December 12, 2006. Eleven men were implicated in the thefts of nearly 300 Hummers and Cadillac Escalades from Miami to Lake Worth in Florida.

The operation based in Miami-Dade County, revolved around an elaborate system in which the men altered vehicle identification numbers of stolen General Motors SUV's before they shipped them out of state to be resold. "This case has stretched out to so many places across the country, it is unbelievable." A Miami-Dade Auto Task Force detective said.

The ring was led by Carlos Ponce, known in South Florida crime circles as "the King of Cars" and the investigation led to more than 50 arrest in 20 states. Antoine Ferrer, another principle in the ring, who cooperated with authorities, gave up Fat Cat and Richard "White Boy Rick" Wershe. Both of the street legends were serving time in the federal Witsec Program at FCI Mariana in Florida.

Ferrer told Wershe about the deal by phone, investigators said, and they worked with Fat Cat to ship more than a dozen SUV's to his son Lorenzo Nichols Jr. in Virginia Beach, Virginia, where the younger Nichols sold them to his associates. "They're just a small part of the overall case," the detective said. "But we couldn't do this without closing the loop on them too."

Inmates Ran Stolen Car Ring, the *Miami Herald* headline read on December 13, 2006. Detectives found pictures of some of the fancier cars in Nichols federal prison cell. "White Boy Rick and Fat Cat, they were responsible for one or two of the routes that cars went up north," the detective said. From his cushy cell in the Witsec Program the Cat allegedly helped move over $8 million in cars stolen in South Florida between 1999 and 2005.

For his role in the car theft ring, Cat was sentenced to 10 years in prison to be served after he completes his two 25-to-life sentences for drug trafficking and the murder of his parole officer and his 40 years in the feds for two other murders. His son pleaded guilty and was sentenced to seven years.

"He took the beef for the car shit and did nothing." The former Witsec prisoner says. "Didn't get one cent but he made sure his son got probation and in reality his son was running the cars to all his little street buddies. True thug. The BOP used the car thing to throw Cat out of the program. It was a way to get rid of him. As one law enforcement official said, 'If anyone should have received prison time it was Lorenzo Nichols Jr.' But Cat wasn't going for that.

"Cat was used as a pawn to bring publicity to the case. The whole case was 100 percent bullshit. His son bought like six or eight cars and sold them to his street buddies. Next thing you know in 2004 the car guy in Miami gets arrested and in 2005, a year later, Cat and the others get arrested. The dude got busted and gave Fat Cat's name, said he was running it, to get the feds interested and take the heat off his back. Cat wasn't running no car theft ring and neither was his son."

One of the cop killers was back in the news also. *Officer's Killer Wins Lawsuit for Time Spent in Solitary Cell, The New York Times* headline read on February 12, 1999. A federal jury in Rochester, New York found that the inmate, David McClary, had suffered mental stress during the time that prison officials kept him locked up in a tiny cell and that his civil rights had been violated.

Prison officials said that the notoriety of McClary's crime made it necessary to segregate him from other inmates. The jury decided that prison officials were within their rights for initially putting McClary in 23 hour a day lockup, but violated his rights by his continued confinement there. McClary's years in solitary confinement were spent in Attica, Wende and Elmira. McClary was awarded $660,000. Cops were outraged.

"I can't believe it," a Queens detective said, "I heard about it on the exact anniversary of Eddie's murder. I heard a mention of some cop killer getting this big award and a picture of the killers face. Then on the 11 o'clock news there was David McClary, 11 years older than on the day we arrested him for Eddie's murder.

"Eddie never had a chance. It sat me back on my heels. It was a cowardly killing. Poor Eddie didn't even have the chance to look his killer in the eye. They snuck up from behind his car, fired into the window, which shattered and then kept on firing. This was done by people who don't deserve to be called men. I'd like to know this, where are we headed when a killer gets paid by the state for killing?"

The cop killing signaled the end for both Fat Cat and Pappy Mason and served as the primary catalyst for the ratification of the National Crime Bill in 1989. President Bush wore the slain officer's badge and Congress enacted the crack laws. On December 3, 1989, *Newsday* marked the end of the 80s with an article, *The Decade When Queens was King*, that perfectly captured the moment.

The Anti-Drug Abuse Act of 1988, along with creating a cabinet level drug czar, offered harsher punishments for drug offenses, including mandatory minimums in prison for the simple possession of five grams of crack, a twenty year mandatory minimum for a continuing criminal enterprise and the death penalty for drug traffickers who intentionally killed any federal law enforcement officer during or related to a federal drug felony.

Fat Cat and Pappy Mason's actions were directly responsible for the War on Drugs and America turning into incarceration nation. Their reckless exploits and disregard for the law pushed the envelope with law enforcement officials, creating a backlash that hundreds of thousands are still paying the price for today.

Byrne's death did not usher in a new era of killing of law enforcement officials as Congress and the White House feared. Instead it was a signpost that the most intense violence of the crack era was finally coming to an end. Even high ranking members of Fat Cat's organization had grown weary of the violence and were furious with Pappy's actions for ordering the Byrne hit, which they rightly viewed as bad for business.

There would be no Pablo Escobar's in the United States, killing police, prosecutors and judges at his whim, to terrify citizens and create a narco state. The feds, by handing out increasingly harsher punishments, saw to that.

Call it an overreaction to crime, but the feds did what they thought was necessary at the time to stop the violence against law enforcement. They took no chances that it would spiral into another epidemic and rightly so. But the laws they created have imprisoned millions for decades of their lives, destroying families and communities the same as the crack epidemic.

In 1988, declaring Officer Byrne's death "an attack on society," Mayor Edward Koch created the Tactical Narcotics Team to sweep the city's worst drug areas with waves of so called buy and bust operations. South Jamaica became a symbolic outpost in this widening war, a confrontation where brute police force would be marshaled against an entrenched enemy.

As South Jamaica went, so would the drug war the thinking was. TNT made South Jamaica a national symbol in the War on Drugs and its residents couldn't decide which side was winning. In the eye of the storm, it seemed everybody lost.

Thousands of arrests later and the results have been decidingly mixed. Residents, community leaders and the police said that at the very least, social order was restored to the streets that once buzzed with the commerce of crack. They claimed victory because there were fewer wild shootouts over turf and fewer drug dealers operating openly on the streets.

The big drug organizations were broken, their leaders imprisoned. But there was a deep sense in South Jamaica that much of the change had been superficial. The deeper problems were not addressed. There is still drug addiction, crime and poverty in New York City and other areas across the nation.

"I live here and I see it 24 hours a day," a local said. "No matter how much the police do, it seems they can't eradicate it." To walk through South Jamaica, a neighborhood of 42,000 that moves to an unexpectedly suburban rhythm is to see a community deeply scarred by the crack epidemic.

Many residents have lost friends and relatives to the drug game and the violence it spawned, many still refuse to speak openly about drug addiction or dealing out of fear or retribution. This is the legacy of Fat Cat and Pappy Mason.

"They say cats have nine lives, but they killed all nine of this one," the local said. Situated about five miles north of Kennedy International Airport, South Jamaica is a mixture of tidy wood frame houses, public housing, tire strewn lots and factories.

The 1990 Census painted the picture that 90 percent of South Jamaica's residents were black and that 20 percent lived below the poverty line and received public assistance, but most were middle class and lived in one family homes.

Under Fat Cat and Pappy's reign the neighborhood led all Queens precincts in murders and arrests. With their imprisonment, others just took their place. "You have a lot of individual wheelers and dealers, but you don't have a Pappy Mason or Fat Cat anymore," the local said. They were gone, but their infamy remained. In the Southside of Jamaica Queens the names of Fat Cat and Pappy Mason could still stop a conversation cold.

The outcome of the case has been a sensitive topic, even up until today. Cat's stature and legend in the annals of the drug game, has been hotly debated and questioned. To some, Cat is a magnanimous figure who sacrificed himself for those he loved, but others suspect him of assisting in the conviction of his right hand man Pappy Mason and therefore dismiss him as a snitch. Maybe 50 Cent said it best in *Ghetto Qu'ran*, *As a youth, all I ever did was sell crack/I used to idolize Cat/Hurt me in my heart to hear that nigga snitched on Pap/How he go out like that?*

CHAPTER 10

The Debate

*The mind activation/React like I'm facin'/Time like
Pappy Mason/With pens I'm embracin'. Nas, The
World is Yours, Illmatic (1994)*

The issue of Fat Cat being a snitch has been hotly debated
with both detractors and supporters making their cases for or
against. Based on the facts, such as reputable newspapers like *The
New York Times* reporting that he was cooperating, it seems there
is no question of his culpability.

But there is no evidence that Fat Cat ever testified at anyone's
trial. And the true definition of a rat is someone that gets on
the stand and points fingers at his comrades. In prison they talk
about paperwork, and by that they mean transcripts from court.
Actual documentation.

The newspaper can print anything, and be used as a
government propaganda tool, but paperwork from the court
can't lie. But if Cat is not a snitch, how can the fact that he was
in the federal Witsec Program from 1990 to 2006 be explained?
In the streets during those times, dudes knew where Pappy was
at, they knew were Prince was at, they knew were Preme was at,

but no one knew where Cat was.

Prisoners in the federal Witsec Program have their locations closely guarded. The information isn't available to the public. In purely black and white terms that is a big strike against the Cat. But things in life are hardly black and white.

"People like to think of the world in terms of black and white, but most things and answers reside in a broad grey area and Cat's story is no different." Curtis Scoon said. "What I know is in 21 years not one piece of paperwork has surfaced with his name on it. No one can say he testified in court and he's still in prison. There are people walking the streets because Cat did not tell on them and no one can say they're in prison because of him."

This could all be true, but it's also evident that Cat played ball with the feds. Maybe he thought he could outsmart them or trick them, only tell them what he wanted. Who knows? He was probably very selective in what he said to them, and if he only told on himself then what is the crime? But in convict and street terms, everything is black and white, there are no grey areas, you don't talk to the police period.

A litany of street legends who are rats have been glorified in movies, magazines and documentaries including Rayful Edmond, Alberto "Alpo" Martinez, Frank Lucas and Leroy "Nicky" Barnes. The street magazine *F.E.D.S.* has made their mark profiling and interviewing snitches, giving them a forum for their stories.

Just as *Don Diva* magazine has become a forum for the dudes who didn't snitch. It's all urban crime lore, just from a different perspective. To the public, it's all entertainment. But to the dudes doing life in the pen there's a big difference. In prison and the streets the ideals of death before dishonor and omerta are cherished.

Still Hollywood loves a snitch who tells it all, just look at Mafia turncoats like Henry Hill and Sammy the Bull, who sold their stories of betrayal and larceny for big money. In Hollywood it doesn't matter if you are a snitch. Only the story matters. The fact remains that Fat Cat is a legend no matter how much his detractors hate it and for whatever reasons.

"Lorenzo 'Fat Cat' Nichols is a gangster in the true sense of the word before anything else," Curtis Scoon said. To this day, dudes from Cat's crew are loyal to him. Luc Spoon has managed to hold down the name the best he could. The snitch factor has plagued him and other Cat supporters for years, but they've gone through great lengths to clear it up.

Luc Spoon turned to the person that the streets, prosecutors and even 50 Cent said Cat snitched on, Pappy Mason. From phone conversations to countless letters he questioned Pap. Pap denied that Cat ever told on him.

"Quote me on this, Cat told me he told on nobody, Pappy told me 'Cat didn't testify, nor was he in any of his paperwork.' Any real nigga from that era knows ain't nothing come back to haunt them. What rat you know that's never coming home." Luc Spoon said. Maybe a rat that pissed the feds off. But still Luc Spoon has a point, even Sammy the Bull with his 19 admitted murders got out after five years and Cat is still in and most likely never coming home.

To understand the paperwork concept in prison you have to understand how indictments and convictions come about. Before someone is indicted the feds have grand juries. At these grand juries prosecutors lay out their cases against individuals they are targeting and their accomplices. Co-conspirators, police and witnesses testify to the grand jury by answering the prosecutor's leading questions about the targets criminal behavior.

All proceedings are recorded by a court reporter and the transcript made is used as support to get the indictment. Most of these grand jury sessions are secret, closed and not open to the public. The records are usually sealed. But when the targeted individual goes to trail he can get the grand jury statements and transcripts in his discovery materials.

That is the first time when a defendant knows who is really snitching on them. The paperwork is the proof. In prison, paperwork proves someone is hot or a snitch. Without the proof, there's always a question mark. Without the proof, you can't put it out there. You can think what you want, but to broadcast it you need proof. That's how it works on the inside.

The only other paperwork that would indicate someone is a snitch would be court transcripts from trial proceedings, sentencing minutes, pre-sentence investigation reports and judgment and commitments. From any of these documents someone can either be cleared or identified as a snitch. It's all in black and white, and this is what prisoners go by.

When paperwork is produced on someone it can get them checked in or killed. Unless they have paperwork that is verifiable and uncorrupted, convicts in the pen don't usually put jackets on dudes, because that can be a serious miscalculation with deadly repercussions. If you put a snitch jacket on someone that turns out to be false, it can be your ass.

So in truth, besides the newspaper reports, the only paperwork produced on Cat has been his plea agreement. A lot of people sign plea agreements that say they will do this or do that, the paperwork that backs that up to see if they really followed through, is named above. So who knows if Cat made a deal with the feds and never followed through?

Maybe he played them and got himself put in the Witsec Program, where the conditions are plusher and he didn't have to deal with the haters, crackheads and bammers. Maybe that was Cat's angle. Only he knows and he isn't saying. So the question is still up in the air.

The most important thing is what his codefendants say and Pappy Mason doesn't call him a snitch. "I love my brother Fat Cat from Queens," Pappy said. "They lie on Fat Cat and me, word to mother. Cat never testified against me. His name is not in any of my paperwork, he's my brother and I'm his keeper."

A lot of people have always been under the impression that Fat Cat betrayed Pappy, but Pap still calls Cat his brother and says that he never testified against him or was in his paperwork. But the *F.E.D.S.* interview, where Pappy made those statements, has been called into question.

Wayne Perry, the notorious Washington, DC hitman, who is in ADX Florence with Pappy says, "Bro, if it's an interview out on Pappy, trust me bro, Pappy ain't do it or write it. I don't respect or care for a lot of New York cats, but Pappy and Supreme are honorable men."

Lance Fuertado of Seven Crowns fame defends Cat though, "The only person Cat ever told on was himself and he did that to save his mother." A noble cause if there ever was one, but still the accusations linger. But Cat has plenty of backers.

Shocker puts it to rest, "First and foremost, I have nothing but love and respect for Fat Cat, because he always showed me nothing but love. Now with that being said, yes, I've heard the rumors and whispers about him rolling over, but he didn't get on the stand at my trial or anybody else's trial in my case, nor did he say anything incriminating about me or Pappy so far as I know. I haven't seen any paperwork, so I'm not going to put a bad bone on him." Cat stands up for himself also.

"Who did I tell on?" Cat questioned. "Some of these guys have to talk about me because they have no meaningful history of their own. They want to be something they're not. If they want the crown, they can have it. I'm done with it."

Even though Pappy Mason sticks up for his man, street legend discredits Pappy, due to him being shot up with Thorozine. Pappy was always crazy, but after 20 plus years of incarceration, mostly all in solitary confinement, waging a constant battle against prison guards and the demons in his own head, people have said that his condition now is that of a man unfit for reality.

Even Wayne Perry who has been at ADX with Pappy, questioned his supposed *F.E.D.S.* interview where he vindicated Cat, so there are questions all around. But the reality is that Fat Cat remains one of the most infamous gangsters of the black underworld. He is a legendary presence in hip-hop's lyrical lore, no matter what his detractors say. And Pappy sits right there next to him in the chronicles of the gangster pantheon.

"They will forever be linked together," BC says. "For numerous amounts of years dudes have been rapping about Cat ratted on the comrade Pap and got him a life sentence, but Pap spoke the words in the *King* article, 'Cat did not rat on me.'

That should cease all the talk about him ratting. And to seal that officially, the comrade, Lance Fuertado spoke nothing but good things about the homie. So for him to speak so well about Cat as well as Pap, all that shit should finally cease."

F.E.D.S., As Is and *Don Diva* have all covered Fat Cat and Pappy Mason's stories, albeit from different angles. Fat Cat's story has been profiled in *King* magazine, written about in Ethan Brown's *Queens Reigns Supreme* and Mike McAlary's *Copshot*, and been featured on BET's *American Gangster*. The man instrumental in the *King* article, *American Gangster* episode and Ethan Brown's book is Curtis Scoon, and he's been one of Cat's biggest supporters.

"I saw Cat had a need to set the record straight, he trusted me. He got a chance to speak to someone who wasn't going to twist his words and make him look bad. I found out they were doing Fat Cat on BET's *American Gangster* and naturally I wanted to get involved. I was hired as a consultant and I helped them put together a show and they got a lot of access through my participation. I pitched *King* on the Fat Cat story. I got them the exclusive and I wrote the article." Curtis Scoon said.

"There's an unhealthy obsession with Cat in some circles of those who are consumed with jealousy and envy. When I spoke to Prince he couldn't stop saying how much of a rat Cat is, but not once did he mention the rats who testified against him and gave him seven life sentences or tell me who Cat told on. Dudes have been saying Cat told on Pappy and no one thought to ask Pappy because the facts mean nothing to haters. Now that Pappy says Cat didn't tell on him I'm sure they'll have plenty of questions and no answers." He finishes.

The original street bible, *Don Diva*, the most respected magazine in our nation's prisons- where it can mean death to be a snitch- has held to the official line that Cat is a rat. As has Prince from the Supreme Team, who has lots to say about Cat.

Having been in prison for two decades himself, doing all his time in the vicious United States Penitentiaries, Gerald "Prince" Miller had never conducted an interview with any media outlet, until he decided to give *Don Diva* his first ever interview in the wake of what he called BET's *American Gangster* "mockumentary" and the book *Queens Reigns Supreme* on Fat Cat.

"Ethan Brown's book, *Queens Reigns Supreme* and the *American Gangster* documentary on Fat Cat are based upon misrepresentations, half-truths and bold faced lies," Prince said. "The story being told is manipulated by Fat Cat. The puppets only do what the puppeteer commands them to. Cat is only going to let you see of him what he wants you to see.

"Before *Queens Reigns Supreme* came out they asked me to see if I would participate in the book. I got a number and called. They filled me in on what the book was really about and who would be included-Lorenzo 'Fat Cat' Nichols. I declined and specifically told them, 'I'm not going to participate in glorifying a rat.'

"They questioned whether or not Cat was indeed a rat. In response I asked, 'You sure you're from New York?' Before they answered, I said, 'Give me your address and I will send you the proof.' I sent the proof and never heard from them again. When Ethan Brown's book finally came out, none of the paperwork that was sent exposing Fat Cat as an informant was included.

"*King* magazine, in their March/April 2007 issue on Fat Cat, should have taken the time to do the research for the story themselves. Instead they depended on a contributing writer with a hidden agenda to interview Cat and ink the tale, when the advertisement for the BET series *American Gangster* started airing it exposed Nicky Barnes as an informant, yet it spared Fat Cat the same dishonorable title he worked so hard to obtain. I gathered the majority of the documents in my possession and wrote a cover letter to BET.

"The letter and documents were sent to the executive producer for *American Gangster*. I trusted BET would utilize and expose these documents when the program on Fat Cat aired. However when the segment was aired they glossed over the fact that Cat cooperated with the government. Now as for issue 2 of *As Is* magazine, that's a whole different story. The editor-in-chief used to work for *Don Diva* magazine, so he should have been aware of *Don Diva's* previous articles, specifically the one about Fat Cat being an informer and resident of the Witness Protection program.

"You can never truly separate your past from your present. But if you're crafty enough you can manipulate the present to make people forget about your past as their eyes look toward the future. There's an old saying my right hand man, C-Just, once told me, that sums up what's taking place, the truth and the lie had a race, the truth had won, but the lie took its place. The history of South Jamaica, Queens most bold and notorious informer must be recorded for all generations to see. Never to be forgotten."

When someone brought up the subject of Fat Cat being a snitch to Supreme, the leader of the Supreme Team and Prince's uncle, he politely refused to comment on the situation. And when Supreme was fighting his 2006 case with Murder Inc. the feds reached out to Fat Cat and asked him to testify against Supreme and Cat told them to kick rocks. That goes to show that everything is not always as black and white as it seems. There are some possible explanations about Cat that have not been explored in this debate.

Fat Cat, being the intelligent person that he is, tried to play the feds. But no one can outsmart the feds or very rarely do, you are either with them or against them. The feds play dirty, everyone knows that. So Cat is still suffering to this day for trying to outsmart them. Is it not possible he told them he would cooperate, with no intentions of doing so, to lighten the load on his mother and other codefendants, many of whom were his female relatives?

It would seem he took a great responsibility on himself in a way, by shifting all the weight and taking the burden off their shoulders. But isn't that what a truly honorable man would do? Or is letting your mother go to trial the way to go? Heavy is the head that wears the crown.

It's easy for others to criticize because their mothers, sisters and other female relatives weren't facing time. It's different going to battle against the feds with a cadre of killers and hardened convicts, than with a bunch of women. It speaks to Cat's sizable reputation that he was even able to keep his organization running from prison, through his female relatives, on the strength of his name alone.

Cat may have seen the hand he was dealt and tried to play it the best he could for other people's benefit, as it's clear he is still in prison and others aren't. He was the sacrificial lamb. Even if he was in the federal Witsec Program, prison is still prison. Not making any excuses for Fat Cat, just trying to come up with a plausible explanation. It's a proven fact that even the hardest, most stone-cold killer will flip, this has happened in many cases, so what is the difference here?

The difference is Pappy Mason, who stayed true to the code of the streets. When held up to Pappy, Cat's ideals don't match up, in a strictly criminal mind frame. That doesn't make Cat less the legend. In fact, he is the greater of the legends. Pappy Mason was just his crazy, gun-toting sidekick. Fat Cat was the empire building, multi-millionaire drug lord.

The Cat's wealth and influence dwarfed his peers and contemporaries. But in his effort to outfox the feds did he fuck himself and sully his legacy? This is the question for the ages. In a game where the only rule is don't snitch; Cat left too many questions to answer. Especially concerning his honor.

There are no questions regarding Pappy Mason. In the criminal world he is the ideal, the one who wouldn't bend or even consider talking to the police or copping out. In a strictly criminal underworld standpoint, Pappy is honored while Cat shamed his legacy. Because to be considered or even suspected of being a snitch is the worst thing someone can be in criminal culture and that stigma can never be removed.

Does that make Cat less of a street legend? No, it only adds to his infamy. The textures and layers of his mystique are complex like Whitey Bulger's, instead of more defined like John Gotti. His story is intriguing, a tale of human failings.

In 2010, Cat's name was still relevant in the multimedia. The man behind the murders of a rookie cop and a parole officer more than 20 years ago should die in prison, the city's top cop told the *New York Daily News*. *Don't Parole Fat Cat Drug Lord, Kelly Urges*, the headline read on March 7, 2010.

Even over two decades later, the Cat is still a news headline. "Nichols should not be paroled, now or ever," Police commissioner Raymond Kelly said. He called the murders "a direct assault on society." Not the kind of words used to describe an informant or cooperator.

"We're strongly opposed to his release," a law enforcement official said. "Officer Rooney was trying to help him make his adjustment back into society, he was trying to help Nichols, and Nichols put the contract out on Officer Rooney. He represents the worst of the greedy, heartless drug dealers on our city streets. He was directly responsible for the assassination of a young police officer just to intimidate a brave citizen/witness who had enough. Nichols should never see the light of day again."

On May 27, 2010, Fat Cat responded in the *New York Daily News* by letter. "I came to prison a brazen young man in my 20s and now I'm a humbled middle-aged man of 51." He wrote. "I have nothing but time to ponder my mistakes, to the victims of my criminal activities I offer my deepest apology.

"I'm going to waive my right to appear in front of the parole board. I want you to know I have no expectations of ever being released. I've accepted the consequences of the life I once lived and the choices I made so very long ago. I guess I'm writing to assure you and all who need to know I'm suffering, that my family and I are continually paying for crimes real and imagined."

A law enforcement official dismissed Fat Cat's missive as "an apology of convenience." He went on, "We can't go back in time and resurrect all the victims of this murdering mutt. The only reason he stopped bringing death by guns and drugs to our streets is because we arrested and jailed him."

Over two decades have passed, and because of Cat's street fame and notoriety in hip-hop culture he is still reviled by mainstream society and law enforcement. They detest him and can never forgive him his crimes. But as the magazine profiles, documentaries and hip-hop songs that celebrate his and Pappy's names continue, their place in modern day urban outlaw lore is secure. As two of the biggest street legends from the crack era, they will be forever remembered, glorified and romanticized.

In February 2013, the *New York Daily News* was still reporting on Pappy Mason, the Bebos and the Edward Byrne story. *High-Ranking Bebos member Responsible for Queens Crack Epidemic Will Serve Maximum Sentence*, the headline read. The story was on Char "Shocker" Davis and reported how a Brooklyn federal judge rejected a bid to reduce Shocker's 33 year sentence for being a part of the Fat Cat/Pappy Mason case.

The *New York Daily News* quoted Shocker from an interview he did on Gorilla Convict. Judge Korman, still on the bench told Shocker, "The sentence I imposed was driven as much by the need to incarcerate a dangerous defendant as well as one who was intimately involved in the violent crack epidemic that plagued New York in those years." It seems the Big Apple will never forget.

Call Fat Cat what you will, his name is still larger than life. And with BET's *American Gangster* series producer Curtis Scoon pushing a movie on Fat Cat, Pappy Mason and the Edward Byrne killing, the Cat is about to go Hollywood. It's rumored 50 Cent or Ice Cube are looking to play the lead in the film, titled *Officer Down*. Wacka Flaka Flame has also been rumored to be interested in playing Pappy Mason.

Fat Cat is a certified ghetto superstar and urban icon. Out of the constellation of hood stars in the Queens sky, he was the one who most definitely shined the brightest. A drug kingpin and straight gangster who ruled an empire and commanded killers like Pappy Mason, his second-in-command.

Howard "Pappy" Mason was a true soldier in every sense of the word. He out *Scarfaced* Tony Montana. In one of the most violent eras in New York history Pappy rose above the rest to cement his reputation as one of the most feared men in the five boroughs. He was the guy that nobody wanted to fuck with. He was the baddest man on the block.

As Shocker put it, Pappy was, "a gangster god," with the swagger, mystique and props that left other tough guys from the era shook. Along with Fat Cat, Pappy Mason has gone down in the annals of bad guy lore as an infamous gangster and notorious legend of the black underworld.

Sources

King Magazine
Don Diva Magazine
Smoking Section website
As Is Magazine
F.E.D.S. Magazine
Allhiphop.com
Copshot by Mike McAlary
New York Newsday
Queens Reigns Supreme by Ethan Brown
wikipedia.org
New York Daily News
gorillaconvict.com
King of Kings DVD
New York Magazine
The New York Times
Queens Tribune
BET's American Gangster series
The Miami Herald
Street Legends Vol. 1
Court Records
Snitch by Ethan Brown
Stop Smiling Magazine
XXL Magazine
The Source Magazine

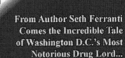
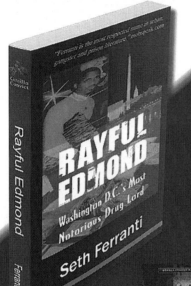

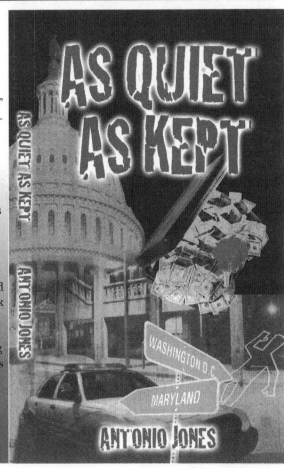

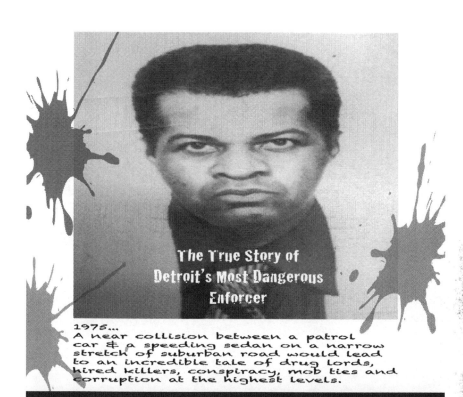

The True Story of
Detroit's Most Dangerous
Enforcer

1975...
A near collision between a patrol
car & a speeding sedan on a narrow
stretch of suburban road would lead
to an incredible tale of drug lords,
hired killers, conspiracy, mob ties and
corruption at the highest levels.

Diary of a Motor City Hitman:
The Chester Wheeler Campbell
Story
by
Christian Cipollini
www.diaryofamotorcityhitman.com

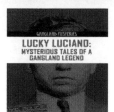

Made in the USA
Middletown, DE
15 January 2017